T0318400

Legal Experiments for Development in Latin America

This book provides a nuanced picture of how diverse legal debates on the pursuit of economic development and modernization have played out in Latin America since independence.

The opposing concepts of modernization theory and Dependency Theory can be seen to be playing out within the field of legal transformation, as some legal analysts define law as a closed, formal, rational system, and others see law as inseparable from economic, social and political change. Legal experiments have followed these trends, in some cases using legal instruments to guarantee classical, civil and political rights, and in others demanding radical transformation of existing legal structures. This book traces these debates across the key topics of: economic development and foreign investment; property; resource and power distribution in terms of gender and social policy. Drawing on a wide range of literature, the book adds complexity and color to our understanding of these themes in Latin America.

This insightful exploration of comparative law within Latin America provides the tools needed to understand legal transformation in the region, and as such will be of interest to researchers within law, political sociology, development and Latin American studies.

Helena Alviar García is Professor of Law at Sciences Po Law School in Paris.

Routledge Studies in Latin American Development

The series features innovative and original research on Latin American development from scholars both within and outside of Latin America. It particularly promotes comparative and interdisciplinary research targeted at a global readership.

In terms of theory and method, rather than basing itself on any one orthodoxy, the series draws broadly on the tool kit of the social sciences in general, emphasizing comparison, the analysis of the structure and processes, and the application of qualitative and quantitative methods.

Welfare and Social Protection in Contemporary Latin America
Edited by Gibrán Cruz-Martínez

Industrial Development in Mexico
Policy Transformation from Below
Walid Tijerina

The Informal Sector in Ecuador
Artisans, Entrepreneurs, and Precarious Family Firms
Alan Middleton

Development Banks and Sustainability in the Andean Amazon
Edited by Rebecca Ray, Kevin P. Gallagher and Cynthia A. Sanborn

Bolivia at the Crossroads
Politics, Economy, and Environment in a Time of Crisis
Edited by Soledad Valdivia Rivera

Legal Experiments for Development in Latin America
Modernization, Revolution and Social Justice
Helena Alviar García

For more information about this series, please visit: www.routledge.com

Legal Experiments for Development in Latin America

Modernization, Revolution and Social Justice

Helena Alviar García

Routledge
Taylor & Francis Group

LONDON AND NEW YORK

First published 2021
by Routledge
2 Park Square, Milton Park, Abingdon, Oxon OX14 4RN

and by Routledge
605 Third Avenue, New York, NY 10017

*Routledge is an imprint of the Taylor & Francis Group,
an informa business*

Copyright © 2021 Helena Alviar García

British Library Cataloguing-in-Publication Data
A catalogue record for this book is available from the British Library

Library of Congress Cataloging-in-Publication Data
A catalog record for this book has been requested

ISBN 13: 978-0-367-35672-9 (hbk)
ISBN 13: 978-0-367-77612-1 (pbk)

Typeset in Times New Roman
by Apex CoVantage, LLC

For Eduardo, Alejandro and Antonio

Contents

Acknowledgments

The themes discussed here are a product of my interaction with many students, academics, friends and family. I would like to thank a few, with the knowledge that many will be left out.

Janet Halley, David Kennedy, Duncan Kennedy, David Trubek and Lucie White are intellectual role models and academic mentors whose work constantly inspires me.

Karen Engle, Jorge Esquirol, Günter Frankenberg and Isabel Cristina Jaramillo have been my life-long intellectual companions and friends; with them I have had the honor of advancing many fascinating, enriching projects that illuminate many themes of this book.

I continue to engage with, and be inspired by, friends I made during my years as a doctoral student. Among them Libby Adler, Dan Danielsen, Maximo Langer, Vasuki Nesiah, Ileana Porras, Kerry Rittich, Alvaro Santos, Hani Sayed and Robert Wai.

I would also like to thank my friends and colleagues at Universidad de Los Andes, my academic home for almost 20 years: Juan Amaya, Libardo Ariza, Antonio Barreto, Laura Betancur, Jorge Gonzalez, Diego López, Eleonora Lozano, Ana María Muñoz, Liliana Obregón, Carolina Olarte, Esteban Restrepo and René Urueña.

A younger generation, some of whom were my students, also contributed significantly to this book. Among them Tatiana Alfonso, Lina Buchely, Beatriz Botero, Mariana Díaz, Esteban Hoyos, Tania Luna, Nicolás Parra, Natalia Ramírez and Joaquín Vélez.

Sciences Po Law School has hosted me since 2019 and I am grateful for having found a vibrant academic community that supports my writing. Special thanks to Horatia Muir Watt, Jeremy Perelman, Dina Waked and Mikhaïl Xifaras.

Luisa Meléndez and Luis Enrique Penagos were extraordinary research assistants. I am very grateful for their intelligence, hard work, commitment and solidarity.

Without the care and love of friends and family a project like this one is impossible to fulfill. All my love and gratitude to Carlos Alviar, Catherine Claypoole, Felipe Noguera and Catalina Pizano, Carmiña Muñoz and Luis Fernando Samper, Diana Pinto, Dalia Rabinovich, Deb and Mike Sabin and my life sister Patricia Vélez, who passed away at the beginning of 2020.

This book is dedicated to my husband Eduardo and my sons Alejandro and Antonio.

Introduction

At least since independence, ruling elites, citizens and academics in Latin America have been searching for ways to transform the political, economic and social conditions that characterize the region. Behind this aim, lies a conflictual relation with European powers and the United States. For many, transforming meant rejecting Spanish-Catholic influence (which they broadly considered as backward) coupled with eliminating indigenous populations,[1] instead embracing England, France and later along the United States as models to be imitated.[2] For others, there should be a possibility to transform without playing into the civilization/barbarism dichotomy which celebrated everything foreign and attacked all local. This second group of intellectuals and politicians aimed to celebrate the indigenous component and blend it with Western values.

For the first group, the paths that led to civilization were contained in the modernization ideal, which meant reproducing the cultural, social and economic conditions that led to the industrial revolution in Europe. Politically, modernization meant establishing a democratic political system, where civil and political rights are protected, there is formal equality and respect for the rule of law. Most constitutional and legal reforms of the late nineteenth and early twentieth centuries were directed toward establishing these conditions.[3] Economically, it translated into structuring market-type interactions where citizens were not bound by feudal-type relations and were free to work where they pleased, acquire salaries and establish the businesses they desired. Socially, it is illustrated by secularism in public and private spheres, importantly in familiar relations.[4]

The modernization ideal contained the belief that if countries in the region followed a specific path, eventually they would progress and transform. To be sure, there was never complete consensus on how forcefully or universally these elements should be incorporated into national systems. Up to this date, there are still debates regarding the exercise of rights; the elimination of feudal-type relations in the countryside; the incorporation of peasants and informal workers into the market; and the diminishment of the power of Catholicism in familiar relations, including women's access to abortion and same-sex marriage among many others.

On the other side of the political spectrum and developed during the mid-twentieth century, Dependency Theory provides a different interpretation and goal. For Dependency theorists, the starting point is a critique of the modernization ideals. They are particularly critical of the ahistorical analysis it proposed, discounting the long-lasting effects of colonialism. Spanish conquest had social, political and economic effects that were not going to change with constitutional transformations, secularization or the promise of market interaction. As long as countries in the region produced single agricultural or mineral products, there would continue to be unequal relations between core and periphery. In addition, focusing growth on a single product brought a range of problems: roads were designed only for export, not for local needs; a small white elite benefitted economically at the expense of the indigenous and black population, and countries were at the mercy of external demands for a specific product. Germane to this interpretation is the idea that even though politically autonomous, these countries continued to depend on Europe and later the United States. From this perspective, no matter how many modern institutions were set in place, as long as these dependent relations existed, countries around the region would continue to be poor. The essential insight of this group of theorists is as follows: underdevelopment is not a stage previous to development, it is a product of the unequal relations of power. Given this diagnosis, the solution was to de-link from global exchange and start trade with countries that were similarly situated geographically, politically and economically.

There is still another version of claiming difference and separation that is exemplified in the *indigenista* movement. For *indigenistas*, a considerable proportion of citizens (in countries like Bolivia, Ecuador, Guatemala and Honduras) have been either physically eliminated, forced to assimilate or excluded from the rights and privileges that white citizens have. Their proposal is to design constitutions, laws and public policies that are inspired by aboriginal ways of viewing the world.

This book is in part aimed at unveiling the diverse forms that this interaction took, from imitation to separation, specifically in the relation between law and development. As a consequence of this search, the region has been the ground for multiple legal experiments designed to reach goals of modernization and economic transformation. The book describes the legal experiments that accompanied this search, focusing on those aimed at simply achieving growth or at combining it with a shift in the distribution of power and resources. In order to do this, the different chapters explore archetypes inspired by the import substitution industrialization model of the mid-century; Dependency Theory in the late 1960s in Cuba or more recently in Bolivia and Venezuela; the neoliberal wave starting with radical reforms in Chile during the 1970s and its adjustments during the late 1990s in Peru and Colombia as well as the indigenous-inspired transformations in Bolivia in the early twenty-first century.

Bringing in literature

Each chapter starts with a reference to literature. Including excerpts from novels has many justifications. First, it is intended to provide an esthetic context for the debates, beyond the dryness of documents about law and economic development. Second, short passages from novels are brought in to incorporate themes that are present in the lives of those who are the recipients of economic development experiments: the cruelty of dispossession, the pain of exclusion, the ambivalence of motherhood and how both law and access to resources structure the quotidian. Third, many theoretical insights of this tension between sameness and uniqueness were fleshed out through the arts. Octavio Paz, the Mexican Nobel Literature Prize winner, writes about how the original trauma of the region was one of separation and the longing of being reunited. Paz argues that the fact that we speak the same language makes us the same and different, as language shifts according to the context it inhabits. Being similar and dissimilar forces Latin Americans to engage in a different style of dialogue with Europeans and at the same time provides fertile ground for replicating the conditions that led to Western development and modernization.[5] For other writers, difference and dependence are the starting point. García Márquez, also a Nobel Literature prize recipient, claimed difference and separation as viable projects for the Americas. In his work, he defends the idea that Latin America should not aim to belong to or imitate Europe, rather the continent should separate and design its own path to develop. This local design would have to entail broad income redistribution and state-led development.[6]

Both law and literature share the objective of describing, translating and capturing reality through words. Elena Ferrante, the author whose work frames Chapter 3, crystallizes the power of storytelling in the following passage:

Telling stories really is a kind of power, and not an insignificant one. Stories give shape to experience, sometimes by accommodating traditional literary forms, sometimes by turning them upside down, sometimes by reorganizing them. Stories draw readers into their web, and engage them by putting them to work, body and soul, so that they can transform the black thread of writing into people, ideas, feelings, actions, cities, worlds, humanity, life. Storytelling, in other words, gives us the power to bring order to the chaos of the real under our own sign, and in this it isn't very far from political power.[7]

Thus, the excerpts from novels presented in this book illustrate complex and nuanced views of law or its absence. Legal absence describes countries or regions in Latin America where the law does not apply, where there is a legal vacuum that is filled by a landowner, a dictator, a foreigner. Short quotes introducing Chapters 1 and 2 represent this interpretation of law. The opposite view would be law as an accomplice of domination. From this perspective, law serves the owners of the means of production who control legislative, executive and judicial powers. Thus, inequality is not resolved by strengthening the rule of law or expelling foreigners to enforce local regulation. The reference to *One Hundred Years of Solitude* that frames Chapter 5 is an example of this perspective. In sum, literature is a medium through which the tensions, difficulties and nuances of law and economic development policies are exposed. It is also the space that narrative has in law and legal arrangements: how we encapsulate our identity – citizen, peasant, working woman, mother, welfare recipient; how we chronicle the harm inflicted by others in legal terms; the choices we make to escape or abide by law.

The role of law

What role law played or should play in this road to development has been highly contested. Some legal theorists in the region consider law a closed, formal, rational system that works to arbitrate disputes among individuals, as well as conflicts between citizens and the power of the state. From this perspective, law is merely a structure within which human interaction occurs; hence, law is not directly associated with social transformation and should not play an instrumental role. For other academics and legislators, law is inseparable from economic, social and political change. According to this view, law is an open and flexible arrangement that is, and should be, constantly influenced by external issues such as economic development ideals, sociological phenomena, resource distribution goals, as well as national and historical contexts.

The book explores different perspectives of law. It focuses on the diverse ways in which the relation between law and development has been deployed. Three interpretations and a critique are included in the text. A first interpretation defended by a group of academics, legislators and policy makers considers the goal of growth or growth and redistribution as easily translatable into legal instruments. This perspective assumes that law is a malleable devise that can easily contain broader economic development objectives.

From this point of view, the definition of development (growth, growth and redistribution or sustainable growth) should be the guiding principle that the legal system should reflect. Thus, changes are set forth mainly through constitutional reform and administrative law, in a very top down approach. An example would be import substitution industrialization, which was mostly set forth through the regulatory power of the executive branch in the form of tariffs, quotas and the protection of certain sectors or industries. In addition, it is assumed that because technocrats have a more precise knowledge about economic development goals, the other branches of government should be deferent to their policy design choices.

Second, there is another way of interpreting the relationship between law and development that starts out with the importance of legal reform as a value in its own right, not as the result of an economic development idea but rather as an enabler of economic development. This approach has a liberal legalist version and a market-centered one. According to the liberal legalist version, the establishment of a liberal democratic rule of law was necessary to reach economic development. In other words, a specific type of law and legal system, on its own, was a previous requirement to reach economic development. Legal reforms were geared toward transforming law into a system where law is universally applied to everyone, citizens influence legal transformation through a democratic process, there is a clear separation of powers and judges adjudicate according to the clearly established rules. Legal education reform played an essential role, because along with the setting up of a classic liberal legal system, future practicing lawyers, academics as well as law professors, and those in charge of policy making needed to have a way of understanding and applying law attuned with these ideals. As a result, there were many initiatives set in place in Latin American countries aimed at changing the way that law was thought of and taught.

The 1990s saw a revival of the idea that legal transformation was desirable on its own, to aid market transactions. It was translated into an increase in interest and research led by the World Bank regarding the relation between rule of law and development. In very broad terms, this meant that Third World countries in general, and Latin American countries in particular, would enhance development if legal institutions worked well. Among these legal institutions was a functioning judiciary; the pillars of private law, which secured transactions and avoided legal unpredictability; as well as guaranteed property rights. Interestingly (or one might say even in a complimentary way), the same decade saw a range of constitutional reforms aimed at including a generous bill of social, economic and cultural rights as a way to guarantee some degree of distribution. The depth, force and effectiveness of these provisions varied greatly and is analyzed in several of the chapters, but it was an important starting point for many countries.

On the other side of the political spectrum, Dependency theorists in the region had faith in public law (constitutional and administrative law) to put in place their transformative agenda. The Cuban, Bolivian and Bolivarian brought changes in the content of most laws, but not necessarily on the way that the relation between law and transformation was thought of or unpacked. Along the same lines, the Bolivarian (in Venezuela) and Bolivian revolutions were basically set forth through a generous bill of social, economic and cultural rights and their corresponding executive branch regulation. Close observation shows how constitutional and administrative law were the main tools deployed by governments on the right and left.

As a consequence, one of the underlying arguments of the book is to illustrate that critical theory insights regarding how law works – its limitations and possibilities – were largely absent from major leftist transformations. Simply changing the content of constitutional documents, legal texts and administrative regulations is only the first step. After modifications – big and small – progressive lawyers, academics, policy makers, judges, activists and law students must continue to observe how the transformation is occurring, where the backlash is gaining ground and how different branches of law interact with each other in local, national and global settings.

Proposed counterpoint: distributional analysis

For the previous interpretations of the role of law, the relevant rules to deal with a specific problem are limited to a single legal field or topic. This book argues that there is a better way to understand the way law works in order to understand its limitations. Legal architecture is composed of layer after layer of reforms as well as regulations that are in constant interaction with each other. Historical background, economic context and the geopolitical space a country occupies frame the possibilities that legal arrangements have to transform society. The different chapters illustrate why it is impossible to separate the public from the private, contracts from criminal law, family law from labor law and the local from the global.

The proposal is to view the content of law as a product of a dynamic relationship, an ongoing struggle over meaning. In this sense, it is proposed that law is not a static set of rules that are clearly written, applied in a consistent and predictable way. Rather, it is a battlefield, where at any given moment there are competing interpretations; actors who are trying to promote their particular vision of what it should be; institutions filled with bureaucrats who have discretionary power to decide its content and judges who will disentangle its meaning differently according to their theoretical backgrounds.

The final chapter proposes a set of steps to be taken when analyzing law according to this proposal. Among them are unveiling the different actors along with the ideological frame behind their views of law and development and unpacking how law structures the market and detailing the contradictions and clashes between diverse branches of government. All of this is done to argue that the application or exercise of power granted by law is not natural or invisible, it is determined by specific decisions, political choices at every turn that end up benefitting some and affecting others.

Chapter abstracts

To bring together the different strands just described, the book contains five chapters. The first four analyze one of the following topics: constitutional transformation, property concentration, concerns about gender and access to welfare policies. The themes illustrate different ideological approaches that have characterized the search for economic development and its relation to law.

The analysis of the different topics is not aimed at providing a complete, comprehensive picture of either the region or a specific country. First, because it would be impossible to fully describe the range of laws, regulations and judicial opinions about each topic. Second, because the region is too diverse to be pictured and analyzed in a few pages. Rather, the different subjects are proposed as theoretical archetypes that represent a specific ideological sensibility.

The first chapter analyzes, through the issue of foreign direct investment, how constitutional reforms have been an essential tool to enshrine and hopefully make bulletproof a specific view of economic development. At the same time, it argues that constitutional transformations, including a specific economic model, have been embraced by politicians and legal scholars on the right as well as on the left. Placing such faith in a foundational document has been consistent through time and space, starting in the early twentieth century and reaching to present-day discussions regarding the Chilean constitutional assembly. Economic and social transformation has remained elusive, and the chapter argues that this elusiveness is a result of the interactions between contradictory provisions within the same text, as well as the relationship between constitutional provisions and other legal regimes such as property, corporations, trade and family law. The second part of the chapter brings in the cases of two ideologically opposing governments and their attempts at reforming constitutional texts to stifle democratic deliberation regarding the characteristics and possibilities of a specific economic development model.

The second chapter discusses how, despite diverse constitutional and legal transformations framed within diverse theoretical approaches, unequal distribution of agrarian property continues to characterize most of the region and is central to economic development models. The chapter also looks into the social function of property through the Colombian and Cuban case studies, addresses neoliberal reforms through the lenses of Peru and briefly analyzes collective property – all of which are framed by the novel *Pedro Páramo*.

Exploring these three different theoretical approaches, the chapter concludes that all approaches have had to transform as a result of the demands from either the global context, shifting local pressure or, perhaps, a combination of both.

The third chapter focuses on the relationship between women and economic development, in particular, on the importance of reproductive work. It also analyzes the limits of liberal feminism and the challenges faced by indigenous feminists. It has three main parts: the first focuses on theoretical debates and feminist contributions to development; the second looks into liberal, Marxist and indigenous feminism; the last describes three examples from Latin America, each of which represents one of the schools of thought that the chapter addresses.

The fourth chapter aims to explore the interaction between economic development goals and social policies to argue that distributing social services for the population doesn't happen in a vacuum, it is determined by ideas about growth, the role of the state and the prevalence of the market. It analyzes the Covid-19 crisis in order to propose that export-led growth combined with neoliberal social policy design left the region ill equipped to face a crisis of this magnitude and that the relationship between economic development goals and social policies has greatly limited the scope and breadth of welfare provisions.

The fifth and final chapter looks into the relationship between law and social transformation. In doing so, it starts by the Marxist perspective that argues that law is structurally biased because it is a tool deployed to dominate and exploit the working class and argues against it. Afterward, it moves into ideas about law's inherent neutrality and distances itself from it. The chapter proposes that law is neither a direct instrument to promote change nor an impartial, neutral frame or a rigid cage, that leaves no space for action. Rather, what this final chapter is proposing is that law is indeterminate, it entails more bargaining than adjudication, it is shaped by many forces as well as diverse rules and as a consequence is foundational to the distribution of resources.

Notes

1 Richard Morse, in his account of Latin American identity, describes it as follows: "Whatever opposed the progress of the urban, Europeanized world was to be effaced. Consider the military campaigns against 'natives' and backlanders

under General Roca in Argentina and under the Mexican dictator Porfirio Diaz in Sonora and Yucatan and the Canudos war in Brazil." Cambridge: Cambridge University Press, 2008, pp. i–xiv, 4.

2 "Latin American elites, in contrast, apart from intransigent conservative factions or occasional free spirits, were prepared neither to question the implications of Western technology, rationalization and imperialism nor to promote broad consensus on matters of national culture and tradition." Ibid., p. 5.

3 Academic Roberto Gargarella has researched extensively the nuances and differences among Latin American constitutions, demonstrating effectively how despite promising to deliver the premises of the rule of law, many constitutions contained individual rights but the institutional structure they contained granted powers mostly to existing elites and as a matter of fact created the conditions for the deep inequality that characterizes the region. For more on this, see Roberto Gargarella, *The Legal Foundations of Inequality: Constitutionalism in the Americas, 1776–1860* (Cambridge: Cambridge University Press, 2010).

4 For a powerful account on the transformation of family law and relations, see Isabel Cristina Jaramillo, *Derecho y Familia en Colombia: Historias de Raza, Género y Propiedad (1540–1980)* (Bogotá: Uniandes, 2013).

5 "Languages are vast realities that transcend those political and historical entities we call nations. The European languages we speak in the Americas illustrate this. The special position of our literatures when compared to those of England, Spain, Portugal and France depends precisely on this fundamental fact: they are literatures written in transplanted tongues. Languages are born and grow from the native soil, nourished by a common history. The European languages were rooted out from their native soil and their own tradition, and then planted in an unknown and unnamed world: they took root in the new lands and, as they grew within the societies of America, they were transformed. They are the same plant yet also a different plant. Our literatures did not passively accept the changing fortunes of the transplanted languages: they participated in the process and even accelerated it. They very soon ceased to be mere transatlantic reflections: at times they have been the negation of the literatures of Europe; more often, they have been a reply. In spite of these oscillations the link has never been broken. My classics are those of my language and I consider myself to be a descendant of Lope and Quevedo, as any Spanish writer would . . . yet I am not a Spaniard. I think that most writers of Spanish America, as well as those from the United States, Brazil and Canada, would say the same as regards the English, Portuguese and French traditions. To understand more clearly the special position of writers in the Americas, we should think of the dialogue maintained by Japanese, Chinese or Arabic writers with the different literatures of Europe. It is a dialogue that cuts across multiple languages and civilizations. Our dialogue, on the other hand, takes place within the same language. We are Europeans yet we are not Europeans. What are we then? It is difficult to define what we are, but our works speak for us." Octavio Paz, "In Search of the Present," Nobel Literature Speech Lecture, December 8, 1990, translated by Anthony Stanton, www.nobelprize.org/prizes/literature/1990/paz/lecture/.

6 "Latin America neither wants, nor has any reason, to be a pawn without a will of its own; nor is it merely wishful thinking that its quest for independence and originality should become a Western aspiration. However, the navigational advances that have narrowed such distances between our Americas and Europe seem, conversely, to have accentuated our cultural remoteness. Why is the originality so readily granted us in literature so mistrustfully denied us in our difficult attempts

at social change? Why think that the social justice sought by progressive Europeans for their own countries cannot also be a goal for Latin America, with different methods for dissimilar conditions? No: the immeasurable violence and pain of our history are the result of age-old inequities and untold bitterness, and not a conspiracy plotted three thousand leagues from our home. But many European leaders and thinkers have thought so, with the childishness of old-timers who have forgotten the fruitful excess of their youth as if it were impossible to find another destiny than to live at the mercy of the two great masters of the world. This, my friends, is the very scale of our solitude." Gabriel García Márquez, "The Solitude of Latin America," Nobel Literature Speech Lecture, December 8, 1982, www.nobelprize.org/prizes/literature/1982/marquez/lecture/.

7 Elena Ferrante, "A Power of Our Own," *The New York Times*, May 17, 2019, www.nytimes.com/2019/05/17/opinion/elena-ferrante-on-women-power.html?re ferringSource=articleShare

Bibliography

Ferrante, Elena. "Elena Ferrante: A Power of Our Own." *The New York Times*, May 17, 2019. www.nytimes.com/2019/05/17/opinion/elena-ferrante-on-women-power.html?referringSource=articleShare.

García Márquez, Gabriel. "The Solitude of Latin America." *The Nobel Prize*, December 8, 1982. www.nobelprize.org/prizes/literature/1982/marquez/lecture/.

Gargarella, Roberto. *The Legal Foundations of Inequality: Constitutionalism in the Americas, 1776–1860*. Cambridge: Cambridge University Press, 2010.

Jaramillo, Isabel Cristina. *Derecho y Familia en Colombia: Historias de Raza, Género y Propiedad (1540–1980)*. Bogotá: Uniandes, 2013.

Morse, Richard. "The Multiverse of Latin American Identity, c. 1920 – c. 1970." In *The Cambridge History of Latin America, Volume 10: Latin America since 1930: Ideas, Culture, and Society*, edited by Leslie Bethell, I–XIV, 4. Cambridge: Cambridge University Press, 2008.

Paz, Octavio. "In Search of the Present." *The Nobel Prize*, December 8, 1990. www.nobelprize.org/prizes/literature/1990/paz/lecture/.

1 Enshrining economic models into the constitution

In October 2019, citizens filled the city of Santiago to protest a small rise in the fee of public transportation. For days and days, they took to the streets demonstrating their deep discontent with a highly unequal country where 1% of the population earns 33% of the country's wealth (PNUD 2017), a privatized pension system excludes most and the average salary is 540 US dollars (Taub 2019). Interestingly, the majority agreed that what was needed was constitutional reform. They argued that the neoliberal Constitution of 1988 (which, although amended several times, had not been substantially transformed after the democratic transition) was essential in structuring wealth concentration, inequality and the precarious living conditions of many. As a councilwoman said in Chile: "We want a constitutional assembly to write a new constitution, one that prioritizes the lives of human beings above private property" (McGowan 2019).

This chapter argues that the trust in constitutional reform as a magic wand that will solve national problems has been embraced by both politicians and legal academics on the right as well as on the left. As Günter Frankenberg proposes in his comparative study of constitutions:

> For over 200 years constitutional projects have oscillated between the poles of magic and deceit, depending on how ideology, myth and the symbolic dimension come into play. Constitutional magic appears in different guises.
>
> [. . .]
>
> These declaratory acts do something as they declare or constitute, they are performative: they communicate ideas, open up new horizon of meaning and are scripts for events. So it is fair to say that it is not the people who create the declaration or constitution but the declaration or constitution that creates the people.
>
> (Frankenberg 2019)

There is a deeply engrained belief that foundational documents epitomize the spirit of a nation, outline utopia and establish rules for political, social and economic struggles. This partly explains the role of constitutions, for sure. Nevertheless, and as Frankenberg brilliantly lays out in his book, they are also documents used as performance instruments geared toward limiting democratic debates about how to run the economy, configure society or allow political participation. This chapter proposes that placing such faith in the power of constitutional law can partly explain why many of the promises contained in the texts have been elusive for both the left and the right. This elusiveness is the result of turning a blind eye to the interactions between contradictory provisions within the same text, as well as the relationship between existing constitutional provisions and other legal regimes such as property, corporations, trade and family law.

In order to analyze the enshrinement of economic development ideals in foundational texts, the chapter analyzes the regulation of foreign direct investment in several Latin American constitutions. The objective is to flesh out three different theoretical strands that have been prevalent in the region: neoliberalism, the social and the dependency/indigenous influence. These ideological archetypes are different from those proposed by Roberto Gargarella regarding the evolution of constitutions in the region during the nineteenth century. In his very sophisticated work, Gargarella lays out three ideological types: "conservative characterized by the defense of political elitism and moral perfectionism; majoritarian or radical constitutions that sought to reach out to the popular sectors and anchored themselves in a form of moral populism; and individualist or liberal constitutions" (Gargarella 2004, 142). Although I find his work compelling, I am interested in the economic dimensions and manifestations of foundational texts and their relation to economic development goals and ideals.

For the purpose of this chapter, foreign direct investment is "the ownership of productive assets by a parent corporation in another nation. Such ownership should be distinguished from the purchase of foreign stocks or the lending of funds to foreign companies and government" (Cypher and Dietz 2004, 437). It provides a useful template for the analysis of the political economy of constitutions because of the relevant role it has played in discussions regarding economic development. In fact, the embrace or prohibition of foreign capital in Latin America is a theme where one can understand the region's relationship to its colonial past, quest for modernization, theoretical debates about development and uneasy relationship with Western powers. This uneasy relationship embodies contradictory desires and imperatives: a longing to be considered as an equal coupled with a yearning to break loose from the abusive economic ties that continue to compromise the autonomy of the region.

This faith in the power of constitutional texts is further explored in the last part of the chapter by analyzing how ruling elites in Colombia and Venezuela have attempted – with varying degrees of success – to reform the foundational document in order to set in stone a specific development model: neoliberalism (in the case of Colombia) or Dependency Theory (in the case of Venezuela). It ends with a short reflection on what is missing when all faith is placed on constitutional reform.

Foreign direct investment: setting the ground

As I mentioned earlier, foreign direct investment has been a deeply contested topic in the region. On the one hand, it has been deemed necessary to provide initial and much needed capital in poor countries. On the other, it has been depicted as essential to colonial and neocolonial expropriation of resources in the Global South.

A fascinating literary starting point is Rachel Kushner's novel *Telex from Cuba*. In it, the author describes the final period of American foreign direct investment in the province of Oriente in Cuba, shortly before the revolution. It's a riveting account of social hierarchies and the cruelty of discrimination among expats.[1] In addition, it shows that the North Americans who came to Latin America, far from being powerful and dominant figures, were part of the marginalized in their own country and often fled from difficulties at home, which explains why they migrated.[2] It is also an analysis of both the effects that economic domination had on the population and the porous boundaries between the two cultures despite the efforts of foreigners to isolate themselves. Regarding law, the novel clearly shows how US companies had little relevant legal limitations, making their domination and exploitation possible. As the following quote illustrates, foreign direct investment concentrated power and resources in the hands of American citizens who had no duties or commitment to the Cuban people. The sharp inequality meant that the local community received very little in return. In addition, the quote shows the absence of law as central to expropriation:

In Daddy's office at company headquarters there was a big map of Oriente. Oriente was where we lived, and it was Cuba's largest, poorest, blackest province. It has the best climate and most fertile land for growing sugarcane. Castro has it all divided up now, I don't know why; another cockeyed thing like changing the name of our town, Preston, to "Guatemala"– which makes no sense at all. Back then the entire eastern half of the island was all one province, Oriente. On the map in Daddy's office, United Fruit's property was marked in green. Practically the whole map was green – 330,000 acres of arable land – with one small area of gray that wasn't ours marked "owned by others." People have no idea, the scale of things. Fourteen thousand cane cutters. Eight hundred fifty railcars. Our own machine shops, to repair every part in the mill. Our own airstrip, two company DC-3s, a Lockheed Lodestar and Daddy's Cessna Bobcat, which he used for hedgehopping – surveying land or popping over to Banes, the other company mill town thirty miles away. We had our own fleet of sugar boats that went back and forth to Boston.

[. . .]

In Cuba, we Americans had our traditions, our own world. The company had a set of arrangements with Batista, annual payments, and in return there were no taxes, no tariffs, and we didn't have to bother with the labor unions or any labor laws. We exported raw sugar up to Boston for processing, to the Revere Sugar Refinery. Batista came to our house. He and Daddy got along fine. I don't know that they were friends exactly, but they had an understanding.

(Kushner 2008)

This depiction of far-reaching power and the capacity or incapacity of law to reign in is at the center of the debate regarding foreign investment in the region. From a theoretical point of view, the existence of international capital can either be considered essential to development and promoted as much as possible, understood as an important factor that needs to be regulated or forbidden in order to promote national sovereign production (Uprimny 2011).

Ideas about economic development: at the center of the debate

Since the early 1990s, most Latin American countries have changed their constitutions (Uprimny 2011). These new charters aimed to respond to the lack of political representation by traditional political parties, stark levels of poverty as well as unequal distribution of resources across race, ethnicity, class and gender.[3] Theories of economic development have been central to the search for the legal tools to change societies. In this section, three ideas about economic development set forth in the region are discussed: neoliberalism, the social and Dependency Theory with a pluri-ethnic ethos.

Neoliberalism, a fever that started in Chile

Starting during the late 1980s in Chile and then followed by many countries in the region a set of policies was generated that followed the tenets of neoliberalism. Latin American neoliberalism propagates a critique of both the "excesses" of state-led development – most importantly, import substitution industrialization – and of social policies aimed at redistributing resources through food and gas subsidies as well as the provision of basic services such as water, electricity, health and education.

The neoliberal agenda entailed a range of policies, but for the purposes of this chapter, it meant diminishing the centrality of the state in developmental theory and practice. According to neoliberalism, when the state was central to development policy, spaces were open for public officials to engage in rent-seeking practices, prices were distorted because there was little or no competition and winners were hand-picked by the state.

The solution would be to eliminate state intervention in the economy and to unleash the forces of the market. The market in turn would be the best distributor of resources, because public official discretion would be eliminated and equal competition among different actors would be promoted. Accordingly, if the state is taken out of the picture, resources would be adequately assigned to productive endeavors, prices would signal the true costs of goods and corruption would be eliminated. As the Peruvian case analyzed in this chapter demonstrates, a constitution that enhances the neoliberal agenda embraces the centrality of the market, promotes foreign direct investment with little or no limitations and protects the sanctity of private property.

The social: a middle ground between neoliberalism and state-led development

Not all countries of the region were able, or willing, to embrace neoliberal reforms with all their force. Many of them tried to limit the painful consequences of state absence by establishing a set of provisions that acknowledged government action in many areas of social life and allowed its intervention when market failures occurred. In addition, the distribution of public resources could be set in place for those who could not enter the market, this way preserving some spaces for the public provision of certain services. This middle ground is exemplified by the term *Estado Social de Derecho* enshrined in the Colombian Constitution.

In countries with high levels of poverty and exclusion, such as those in Latin America, this middle ground defended the idea that the state must continue to play a small role in order to help those who cannot enter the market. Here, social and economic rights as well as policies such as conditional cash transfers provided the necessary social safety net.

In sum, the social approach is a middle ground between neoliberalism and state-led development. The starting point, as in neoliberalism, is the individual, and the preferred distributor of resources is the market. Nevertheless, this perspective acknowledges that not all individuals can easily enter the market and that there are market failures that make state intervention necessary at times. Therefore, social and economic rights provide the individual citizen with an avenue to access goods such as health and education.

Dependency Theory with a pluri-national approach

In the region there are several constitutions that have enshrined some of the principles of Dependency Theory. Dependency Theory is a critique of the unequal relations between developed and developing countries. For *dependentistas*, underdevelopment is not a historical stage previous to development; it is a product of the structural dependent relations that countries in the South have to countries in the North. In other words, given the power and resource structure of the world, time or good policies will not help peripheral nations develop. Third World countries will always be characterized by poverty and backwardness because they only produce and export primary goods. Pricing for these products happens in international markets, and foreign companies control their local manufacture and extract all resources, both physical and financial, from local economies. A natural solution to the global unequal distribution of capital is the nationalization of resources in order to promote governmental control of their production and distribution within the country.

Along with the critique of center-periphery relations, Dependency Theory entails a full-scale redistribution of resources to empower citizens who have been excluded by traditional economic development models. This is done through the public provision of basic services such as health, primary and higher education as well as important subsidies for food, water and housing.

In this same line of critiquing the universality and neutrality of traditional economic development models centered upon growth, the Bolivian Constitution includes the incorporation of previously silenced ways of living and understanding progress. At least on paper, this charter is an example of an attempt to incorporate a well-balanced relationship with nature.

In Bolivia, Evo Morales campaigned for years against neoliberal economic policies, which he claimed enriched a small transnational elite and impoverished the indigenous majority (Postero, The Struggle to Create a Radical Democracy in Bolivia 2010). The theoretical tenants of what can be understood as a contemporary decolonizing project four centuries after independence are extremely powerful. This renewed decolonization starts out by rejecting the privilege that Hispanic tradition had in terms of language, class and race, and therefore it is a foundational moment that celebrates the pluri-national character of the nation, demands racial and cultural equality as well as the redistribution of local resources. In addition, it entailed the reconceptualization of natural resources not as commodities but as the common property of the pluri-nation (Goldstein 2012).

The basic aims of this perspective are the redistribution of rural land, both unproductive state and privately owned property, to indigenous communities; the nationalization of private companies in essential sectors of the economy (hydrocarbons and mining) to adequately use the income of their production for national industrialization; a large-scale income redistribution generated by gas and mineral exports as well as administrative and fiscal decentralization to ensure indigenous participation (Tsolakis 2012).

Direct Foreign investment – embraced or rejected?

For neoliberal theory, foreign investment is not only desirable but necessary. It is necessary because developing nations lack physical and capital investment, and this is the essential role that foreign companies play. In addition, through foreign investment there is a transfer of knowledge, product and process technology and organizational innovation (Cypher and Dietz 2004).

From the social perspective, capital and other resources provided by foreign investment are undeniable. Nevertheless, it must be regulated, and the incentives must fall within a context of social and national well-being. A concrete consequence would be that there would be no constitutional prohibition to foreign investment.

Finally, for Dependency Theory it is essential to promote sovereign national development and the widespread redistribution of resources. Foreign capital goes against these aims; therefore, the prohibition or strict control of this type of investment as well as the nationalization of strategic sectors of the economy are essential to this theoretical approach.

Additional criteria to be explored in constitutions

As this section has illustrated, the regulation of foreign capital is framed within the broad theoretical structure and imperatives of economic development. In addition to the ideological underpinnings, and in line with the second objective of this chapter, it is also necessary to explore within the constitutional texts the regulation of other related topics such as ideas about distribution and equality as well as the definition and limitations on property. In the following section, examples of a neoliberal, a social and a dependency inspired charter are discussed. The pictures I present are not a detailed analysis of these constitutions; rather they are ideal types that should be used as a starting point for analysis.

The Peruvian Constitution: neoliberalism with few limits

The Peruvian Constitution contains principles that can be clearly linked to neoliberalism. Peru had reached important levels of growth during the 1960s and 70s, through government provision of social services an increase in public investment, and state control over the production of minerals (de la Barra and Dello Buono 2009). By the late 1980s, many Latin American countries, including Peru, were facing economic stagnation. The 1990 Peruvian elections presented an opportunity to leave behind neoclassical interventionism and embrace a new economic model. The elections set the writer Mario Vargas Llosa (who represented the small intellectual elite) against Alberto Fujimori a first-generation Peruvian (his family migrated from Japan) who appealed to the indigenous and mestizo majority. That year most indicators showed a country with very low levels of social well-being; per capita income had returned to the rate of 1955, foreign debt was high and there was inflation of 3,000% (Lee 2010). Alberto Fujimori, the winner of the elections, laid out a neoliberal model to integrate Peru into the global market (Lee 2010).

Given this context, it comes as no surprise that the Peruvian Constitution of 1993 is a remarkable example of neoliberal principles. In the following sections, ideas about development, property and its limitations, equality and distribution and foreign investment are described.

Model of development and foreign investment

The charter begins by placing the individual at the center of the Peruvian state.[4] In addition, it establishes how economic development will be set forth. Specifically, it provides that the market, privatization and limits on state intervention are the guiding principles of the economy.

In Title III Concerning the Economic System, Chapter I, General Provisions,[5] the constitution determines that freedom of contract,[6] free competition supervised by the state[7] and market principles guide the economy.[8] This means that the state does not play a central role and that the private sector is the motor of the economy. In addition, it includes provisions that determine that public, private and foreign investment should be treated equally,[9] transforming the state-led growth tradition of legally privileging public enterprises.

On the other hand, the constitution established that protectionist measures can only be triggered if another nation imposes them and forces the Peruvian state to do so.[10] This provision is interesting because, at least in principle, it means that the Peruvian state could not freely design policies to protect certain sectors of the economy; it could only do so in retaliation.

There are trade agreements that ban protectionist measures, but, still, including this in the constitution further ties the hands of governmental authorities. A current example is the impossibility to produce certain goods that became unavailable during the Covid-19 crisis.

Property and its limitations

This topic is regulated in Title III, in Chapter III, concerning property, in articles 70 to 73 and in Chapter VI, concerning the agrarian regime and peasant and native communities in articles 88 and 89. Property is defined in its most classical form: as an absolute constellation of rights that can only be expropriated after compensation.[11] Therefore, terms such as its social or ecological function, so central to other charters, are not included. Limitations upon property can only be exceptionally set forth in cases of national security concerns and public interest.

The chapter that concerns the agrarian regime and peasant communities protects both native and peasant production style and guarantees their access to communal property.[12] Despite this protection, research has pointed out that capitalist production coupled with foreign investment have received a preferential treatment. Specifically, in the case of mining, the legislation of Peru enables foreign investors to develop extracting programs in communal lands despite the constitutional recognition of the communal property (Lucero 2009).[13]

Ideas on distribution and equality

The Peruvian Constitution includes a long list of rights linked to the exercise of freedom. It has a short chapter on social and economic rights, which enumerates and develops special protection for children and families, the right to health, the right to education as well as the functioning of public universities, the management of the nation's cultural patrimony and labor rights.[14] The emphasis is clearly on individual freedom and a classical understanding of social provisions that is distant from a transformative, distributive view of rights.

Colombia: between neoliberalism and neoclassical interventionism

During the late 1980s and early 1990s before the enactment of the 1991 Constitution, Colombia, as most Latin American countries, adopted neoliberal economic policies. President César Gaviria Trujillo (1990–1994) was responsible for the acceleration and consolidation of free market guidelines:

favoring a reduction on import tariffs, deregulation of finance, privatization and the creation of incentives for foreign investment.

Within this neoliberal context, the country was embarking in the design of a new constitution that was aimed at dealing with profound inequality, rampant discrimination, as well as the widespread violence triggered by an ongoing internal conflict and drug trafficking. The Colombian Constitution of 1991 promised to be more inclusive for minorities, progressive economically and to provide tools for political participation. This brought as a consequence a charter that was a negotiation between economic neoliberal principles and more progressive views of distribution, taxation and state provision of services.[15]

Model of development and foreign investment

In its first article, the charter defines Colombia as a social state under the rule of law, therefore making society and not the individual the fundamental focus of the constitution.[16]

Ideas behind the model of economic development are regulated in Title XI, On the Economic and Public Finance Regime, Chapter I, General Provisions. As it should be expected, the accent is less on the free market and more on the social context within which the constitution develops. Therefore, the constitution states that free competition entails responsibilities, and corporations – which are the basis for development – have a social function.[17]

The Colombian Constitution does not include an explicit reference to foreign investment and does not establish differential treatment between foreigners and nationals. As a matter of fact, regarding the treatment of foreigners, it follows the general principle of establishing equal treatment for nationals and foreigners.

Property and its limits

The Colombian Charter includes a definition of property that is limited by a social and ecological function.[18] Associative and communal forms of domain are protected, and collective property is established for indigenous and afro-descendant populations. A detailed description of the social function of property is provided in the following chapter.

Ideas on distribution and equality

In line with its mediating spirit between neoliberalism and state-led growth, the Colombian Constitution combines civil and political rights with a generous bill of social and economic entitlements. These entitlements include the right to social security, health, housing, clean environment, recreation, special protection for children, worker's rights, human dignity, the social function of property, education and culture.[19] The Constitutional Court, with varying degrees of force, has adjudicated many of these, providing at times limits to unguarded capitalism and market institutions.

Bolivia: Dependency Theory with a pluri-national approach

The rejection of foreign capital is essential to the Bolivian Charter. During the late 1980s and throughout the 1990s neoliberal policies were set forth in the country, which opened the economy to foreign investment in many crucial sectors, most importantly, hydrocarbons, the essential resource it produced. The consequence of the privatization and dominance of international capital were stark in terms of unequal trade. In the late 1990s and early 2000s Bolivia liberated its hydrocarbons sectors. These liberalizing reforms were promoted and financed by the World Bank, the Inter-American Development Bank and the United States. Despite the fact that the Bolivian government received rents from oil and gas production, the taxes structured by the 1996 hydro-carbons law were biased toward private interests. In addition, and despite the fact that firms needed to consult with indigenous peoples affected by gas extraction, companies did little to include these populations (Perreault 2012).

Neoliberal policies at the time included the weakening of the state provision of social services, the elimination of tariffs that made local agricultural production very expensive compared to the price of imports that flooded the market (Arze and Kruse 2004) (Kohl and Farthing 2006) (Postero, Now We Are Citizens: Indigenous Politics in Postmulticultural Bolivia 2006).

Once Evo Morales got to power, with a strong Dependency/Indigenista discourse, the Bolivian Constitution that he and his movement promoted was designed to move the country beyond dependency on foreign-owned companies that produced and exported gas and minerals, leaving little resources for the country. Along the same lines, the constitution was aimed at transforming the country's economic structure by increasing the production of other goods, including industrial ones; and to establish universal social benefits in order to eliminate inequality.

Thus, the Bolivian Constitution has been described as part of the wave of "transformative constitutionalism." Transformative constitutionalism is a term widely used for a range of reforms of the last 30 years or so. Karl Klare and Dennis Davis, in their seminal article on transformative constitutionalism in South Africa, define it as:

> The Constitution of the Republic of South Africa, 1996 embraces an aspiration and an intention to realize in South Africa a democratic,

egalitarian society committed to social justice and self-realization opportunities for all. The text acknowledges that the new dispensation arose in a particular historical context and that the democracy it inaugurates and celebrates is permanently work in progress, always looking forward, always subject to revision and improvement.

(Davis and Klare 2010)

In the case of Bolivia, the document includes (i) the centrality of the environment and the interconnected nature of the relationship between humans and nature, (ii) the anti-colonial perspective and (iii) its broad definition of property (May and Daly 2013).

Model of development and foreign investment

The model of development set forth by the Bolivian Constitution aims to re-found the nation around novel social, political and economic ideas. In its preamble, the charter distances itself from neoliberalism and neocolonialism, and embraces an interconnected, egalitarian, pluri-national view of society:

> A State based on respect and on the equality of all, on principles of sovereignty, dignity, complementariness, solidarity, harmony and equity in the distribution and redistribution of the social product, where the search for the good life prevails; with respect for the economic, social, legal, political and cultural plurality of the inhabitants of this land; in collective coexistence with access to water, work, education, health and housing for everybody.
>
> We leave behind us the colonial, republican and neoliberal State. We assume the historical challenge to build together a unitary, social, plurinational communitarian state based on the rule of law (*Estado Unitario Social de Derecho Plurinacional Comunitario*) which integrates and articulates the proposals for advancing towards a Bolivia that is democratic, productive, peaceful and peace-inspiring, committed to the integral development and the free determination of peoples.[20]

In addition, in the fourth part, Economic Structure and Organization of the State, the constitution lays out the principles of redistribution,[21] state intervention in the economy to achieve the goals of equality in economic as well as in social terms[22] and the privileging of national production over foreign production.[23] This includes that the aims of the state should be the creation of the conditions to move away from dependence upon the export of hydrocarbons and minerals.

Nevertheless, the charter seems to shy away from fully eliminating capitalism or experimenting with different ways of measuring growth, and at times reads as middle ground as the Colombian one. For example, it provides that economic organization can be "communitarian, state, private and social cooperative."[24] In addition, it describes private initiative and enterprises as central to the economy:

Article 308: I. The State recognizes, respects and protects the private initiative which contributes to the economic and social development and strengthens the economic independence of the country.
II. Free enterprise and the full exercise of business activities are guaranteed and shall be regulated by statute.

Foreign investment is heavily regulated. In this topic, the charter is clearly making a statement. It situates itself outside the embrace of free trade by specifically stating that there is a preference for national production.[25] In addition, the constitution demands that negotiations with the Bolivian state take place in conditions of "independence, mutual respect and equity,"[26] which signals that it is breaking away from a non-distant neocolonial past where economic negotiations with the Bolivian state were taken in conditions of dependency, disrespect and inequality. Autonomy from multilateral as well as financial institutions and transnational corporations also includes the following statement, which all constitutions in the Global South should have:

Article 320 [. . .] **IV.** The State is independent in all its decisions on domestic economic policy, and shall not accept demands or conditions on this policy imposed by states, Bolivian or foreign banks or foreign financial institutions, multilateral bodies or transnational companies.

Property and its limits

The Bolivian Charter places its emphasis on the social dimensions of property. It therefore establishes that every citizen has access to private property as long as it does not go against the collective interest[27] and it gives special attention to peasant production as well as communal and collective property.[28] It states in several places the property of national resources belongs to the Bolivian people and must be used for their benefit:

Article 357   In view of their status as social property of the Bolivian people, no foreign person or company, nor any Bolivian person or private company may register property titles to Bolivian natural resources in stock markets or employ them as means in financial operations aiming at the transfer of assets or their use as security.

Nevertheless, as with the case of ideas about economic development, it does not weaken private property because adequate compensation must follow expropriation[29] and there is a right to inheritance,[30] therefore making radical economic redistribution almost impossible.

Ideas on distribution and equality

As has been clear in the previous sections, the idea of distribution and equality radiates through the whole document. It includes a very generous charter of social and economic rights as well as the recognition of historical grievances of the indigenous population and guarantees legal pluralism, territorial autonomy and provides them with collective rights. The real promise of redistribution lies in the way it understands national property over natural resources and specific social welfare aims to the profit generated by this crucial economic activity.

Protecting constitutional provisions from political deliberations: examples on the right and the left

In this last section I would like to analyze two examples that reiterate the importance of constitutional texts for both right- and left-wing governments. It builds on ideas about neoliberalism and dependency presented previously. It brings an analysis of a Colombian right-wing government trying to tilt a social state frame toward a more neoliberal one by including specific clauses in the constitution. It also describes the steps taken by the Chávez government in Venezuela in order to strengthen the dependency-inspired content of the constitution. Both moves were taken in order to isolate ways to run the economy from political deliberation.[31]

Neoliberal expansion

As I stated earlier, enshrining neoliberal provisions in the region's constitutions included deregulating and privatizing the economy, liberalizing trade and industry, privileging foreign investment and including fiscal austerity.

In Colombia, the constitution has been reformed more than 25 times, many of them geared toward counteracting Constitutional Court rulings that chastened the neoliberal content of the constitution within the frame of social and economic rights, somewhat reframing the power of the market. Neoliberal policy makers strongly opposed limitations imposed by the court. Critics argued that justices were unduly interfering without having the technical knowledge in economic matters or being institutionally empowered to decide over public spending.[32] These critiques led to a constitutional amendment designed to force judges to take into account budgetary restrictions. The article empowered the attorney general or any government minister – once a ruling was handed down from any high court – to make a request to open a "Fiscal Impact Procedure."[33] This procedure could invalidate rulings that heavily affected public finances. The government official who initiates the process has to justify the use of this procedure;[34] the court must respond with a concrete plan for compliance and can change its decision in order to modify or defer the effects of the specific ruling.[35]

The neoliberal expansion can also be seen as a form of governance, in the way that Constitutional Court rulings are implemented. More and more, the language of the market permeates the way the role of the state is understood, exercised and evaluated.[36] Thus, judicial orders often adopt evaluation mechanisms such as cost/benefit analysis, best practices and governance; and use indexes to evaluate policies.[37]

Protection of a dependentista constitution in Venezuela through direct democracy and executive power strengthening[38]

Venezuela provides an interesting ideological counterpoint, with the same faith in constitutional provisions. The first announcement that Chávez made upon assuming power was to propose not one but three referendums: one on whether to rewrite the constitution, a second to elect delegates to the assembly that would be in charge of rewriting it and a third one to ratify it (Krauss 1999). When he inaugurated the sessions of the assembly, he promised the Venezuelan people a radical break from the past. The new foundational document relied heavily on popular participation, assuming, at least initially, that the solutions for social and economic difficulties would come from the bottom up.

The foundational document produced after the Assembly was not as radical as Chávez announced and many elements of the previous constitution remained. Nevertheless, there were important changes that set the initial stages of the Bolivarian Revolution: a longer list of social and economic rights that could be directly adjudicated; the prohibition of selling of shares in the state oil company PdVSA; the establishment of governmental control over pensions (González Cadenas 2020). Paradoxically and despite creating mechanisms for direct political participation – which could bring as a consequence the diffusion of political power – it also strengthened the executive by increasing the presidential period and including the possibility of reelection more than once. It was approved by 71% of the vote in a referendum with a 50% abstention (Canon 2010).

Seven years later, Chávez sought to reform the constitution once again in order to, in his own words, consolidate the socialist state. The themes drafted in 69 articles covered expanding presidential power by augmenting the presidential term to seven years, eliminating limits on reelection and allowing the president to design special military and development zones, curtailing Central Bank autonomy by giving the president direct access to the country's international financial reserves (Krauze 2018). In relation to the management of the economy, it included the strengthening of collective and social property and proposed the elimination of state protection of privately owned corporations (Romero 2007). The amendment also recognized and granted special rights for Venezuelan afro-descendants and banned discrimination on the grounds of sexual orientation (Canon 2010). Despite the fact that Chávez announced that whoever voted *no* was voting in favor of his enemy George W. Bush (Agencia Bolivariana de Noticias 2007), the referendum was rejected by a slim margin: 50.65% against and 49.34% in favor (Canon 2010).

Unable to change the constitution through a referendum, Chávez used a provision that allowed him to replace the legislative branch and legislate certain specific matters. During his presidency, Chávez obtained four habilitating laws (1999, 2000, 2007, 2010) (Arias Castillo 2012). It is interesting to observe how this delegation evolved in terms of scope and length of time. The first one in 1999 established very narrow themes and a term of six months. In 2000, the themes were broader and the period for which it was granted covered a year. In 2007 and 2010 the themes were all encompassing, and the period was extended to 18 months (Arias Castillo 2012). This trend has only increased. Since he took office in 2013, Nicolás Maduro has been granted 53 months to regulate under-enabling laws (Econométrica 2018).

The first law of this type used by Chávez was employed to reform the taxing system: diminishing VAT and new duties. In 2001, the National Assembly delegated in him legislative powers for a second time. This time, the power was used to significantly increase state intervention in various sectors. Among them was an agrarian reform, *Ley de Tierras y Desarrollo Agrario*, where he declared land of essential social interest as well as of public utility; eliminated the possibility of holding big land extensions, *latifundio*; enshrined the ability to intervene in the use of public and private land; and established a publicly owned coastal zone of 260 feet bordering beaches, rivers and lakes. In addition, he regulated fishing, providing special protection for artisanal fishermen; the promotion of small/midsize enterprises and an organic law regulating the oil sector that increased public participation in its ownership and redesigned its organic structure (Armas 2013). By 2007, and after the defeat of the referendum, the scope and breadth of this power was greatly increased. This year the enabling law approved by the assembly included the transformation of state agencies; the strengthening of popular power; social and economic matters; taxing and financial issues; citizen safety; science and technology; geographical and territorial organization; national security and defense; infrastructure, transport and services and the energy sector (Alfonzo Paradisi 2011). It is difficult to imagine what was outside the scope of this law. All in all, these enabling laws in turn produced an extensive array of legislation: 215 in total (Ramirez 2017).

Conclusions

This chapter was meant to illustrate the ideology that structures the economic content of foundational texts in the region: neoliberal, the social and *dependentista*. In order to exemplify the theoretical possibilities, the chapter took foreign direct investment as its starting point. The novel *Telex from Cuba* framed the expropriation and exploitation experienced by local communities in the absence of law. The second part of the text illustrated the lengths to which local elites go in order to defend or deepen further their theories about the economy in constitutions. An overarching theme of this chapter is the generalized faith in constitutional law as central to economic and social transformation.

This faith creates two blind spots. First, it fails to acknowledge tensions within foundational texts, how these tensions will be resolved and who will be called to solve them. The Peruvian Constitution, for example, includes a protection of native and peasant production style and guarantees access to communal property along with a definition of private property as absolute and a privileged protection of foreign investment. Along these same lines, it includes a short chapter for social and economic rights embedded within enshrinement of individual freedom as paramount. In the Colombian case, the tension between a generous charter of social and economic rights and a neoliberal view of economic policy led to at least ten years of dispute between the Constitutional Court and technocrats. In Bolivia, despite its *dependentista* promises, the foundational text shies away from totally distancing itself from capitalism and continues to protect private property. Second, and as discussed in other chapters of this book, constitutional law interacts with other legal regimes such as property or economic development policy in the form of administrative or trade law and this interaction ends up framing the force and breadth of any constitutional provision.

Notes

1 In a critique of the novel published in the *New York Times*, these hierarchies are described as follows: "The expats further separate themselves into classes, represented here by the elite Stiteses, the oddball middle-class Lederers and the violent Allains, poor refugees from Louisiana. Class and race may be, as one character describes the Tropic of Cancer, 'divisions on a surface that is indifferent to . . . borders, that can hold no object in place' – but the only society the Americans can imagine is one based on those divisions, and to them every American's status in Cuba is higher than in the United States." S. Cokal, "Livin la Vida Loca," *The New York Times*, 2008, www.nytimes.com/2008/07/06/ books/review/Cokal-t.html.

2 In another review published in the *Guardian*, this idea that migrants were the losers that fled from all kinds of problems in the United States is explained: "For American expatriates, Cuba is a 'loser's paradise'; many of the adult characters are escaping difficulties and failures at home. They advertise for light-skinned servants (but not albinos – that would be too depressing) and play at being snobs, with golf courses, swimming pools and polo grounds, and all the preening coldness – much of it from women – that snobbery requires. There is also the brutality of the mine and of the sugar mill, the injustices suffered by the indentured workers and the atrocities committed on those workers by America's ally, Batista. 'It was almost Christmastime,' one woman notices, over her cocktail, and there were human beings hanging in the trees beyond the security fence." A. Enright, "Telex from Cuba by Rachel Kushner Review – the Last Days of the Americans," *The Guardian*, 2014, www.theguardian.com/books/2014/apr/23/ telex-from-cuba-rachel-kushner-review?CMP=share_btn_link.

3 Much has been written about the transformative impulse of these constitutions. An interesting perspective is set forth in Boaventura de Sousa Santos, *Refundación del Estado en América Latina. Perspectivas desde una epistemología del Sur* (Lima: Instituto Internacional de Derecho y Sociedad, 2010).

4 Article 1 of the Peruvian Constitution states: "The protection of the human person and the respect of his dignity are the supreme goal of society and of the State." Oxford Constitutions (http://oxcon.ouplaw.com). © Oxford University Press, 2015. All Rights Reserved. Subscriber: Harvard University Library; date: 26 December 2016.

5 Oxford Constitutions (http://oxcon.ouplaw.com). © Oxford University Press, 2015. All Rights Reserved. Subscriber: Harvard University Library; date: 26 December 2016, Articles 58–65.

6 Article 62 states: "The freedom to contract guarantees that the parties may validly negotiate according to the regulations in effect at the time of the contract. The terms of a contract may not be modified by laws or other provisions of any kind. Conflicts stemming from a contractual relation may be adjudicated only through arbitration or judicial decision, in accordance with the procedures of protection provided in the contract or by law. By means of contract-law, the State may establish guarantees and grant assurances. These may not be modified by legislation without prejudice to the protection mentioned in the previous paragraph."

7 Article 61 states: "The State facilitates and oversees free competition. It checks any practice that limits it and the abuse of dominant positions or monopolies. No law or agreements can authorize or establish monopolies." Oxford Constitutions

(http://oxcon.ouplaw.com). © Oxford University Press, 2015. All Rights Reserved. Subscriber: Harvard University Library; date: 26 December 2016.

8 Article 58 states: "Private initiative is free. It is exercised in a market economy. Under this system, the State guides the country's development and acts primarily to promote employment, public health, education, security, public services, and the infrastructure." Oxford Constitutions (http://oxcon.ouplaw.com). © Oxford University Press, 2015. All Rights Reserved. Subscriber: Harvard University Library; date: 26 December 2016.

9 Article 60 in its last line states: "Business activity, whether public or not, benefits from the same legal treatment." In addition, article 63 states: "Domestic and foreign investments are subject to the same conditions. The production of goods and services and foreign trade are free. . . ." Oxford Constitutions (http://oxcon.ouplaw.com). © Oxford University Press, 2015. All Rights Reserved. Subscriber: Harvard University Library; date: 26 December 2016.

10 Article 63 states in its second paragraph: "If another country or countries adopt protectionist or discriminatory measures that prejudice the national interest, the State may, in defense of the latter, adopt similar measures."

11 Article 70 states: "The right to own property is inviolable. The State guarantees it. It is exercised in harmony with the common good and within the limits of the law. No one may be deprived of his property except in the interest of national security or public necessity, determined by law, and after payment in cash of appraised indemnification which includes compensation for possible loss. A claimant may appeal to the courts challenging the assessed value of the property which the State had determined to pay in the expropriation proceedings." Oxford Constitutions (http://oxcon.ouplaw.com). © Oxford University Press, 2015. All Rights Reserved. Subscriber: Harvard University Library; date: 26 December 2016.

12 Article 89 establishes: "The Peasant and Native Communities have a legal existence and are juridical persons.

They are autonomous in their organization, in their community work, and in the use and free disposition of their land as well as in their economic and administrative management within the framework established by law. The ownership of their land is imprescriptible, except in case of relinquishment provided for in the previous article.

The State respects the cultural identity of the Peasant and Native Communities." Oxford Constitutions (http://oxcon.ouplaw.com). © Oxford University Press, 2015. All Rights Reserved. Subscriber: Harvard University Library; date: 26 December 2016.

13 See also Douglas A. McGee and Kwanok Kim, "Constitutions, Economic Policy, and Citizen Support for Democratic Institutions: Peru And the Philippines in Comparative Perspective," *Pacific Focus* 12, no. 2 (2008): 111–38.

14 Articles 4–29, Constitution of the Republic of Peru in: Oxford Constitutions (http://oxcon.ouplaw.com). © Oxford University Press, 2015. All Rights Reserved. Subscriber: Harvard University Library; date: 26 December 2016.

15 For more on this compromise and how it has played out in Constitutional Court rulings, see "Constitución de 1991: El caso de la intervención de la Corte en la economía," in *Hacia un nuevo Derecho Constitucional*, ed. Daniel Bonilla and Manuel Iturralde (Bogotá: Uniandes, 2005).

16 Article 1, Constitution of the Republic of Colombia: "Colombia is a social state under the rule of law, organized in the form of a unitary republic, decentralized,

with autonomy of its territorial units, democratic, participatory, and pluralistic, based on respect of the human dignity, on the work and solidarity of the individuals who belong to it, and the prevalence of the general interest." Oxford Constitutions (http://oxcon.ouplaw.com). © Oxford University Press, 2015. All Rights Reserved. Subscriber: Harvard University Library; date: 26 December 2016.

17 Article 333, Constitution of the Republic of Colombia: "Economic activity and private initiative must not be impeded within the limits of the public good. For their exercise, no one may demand prior permission or licenses without authorization of an Act.

Free economic competition is a right of everyone entailing responsibilities.

The enterprise, as a basis of development, has a social function that implies obligations. The state shall strengthen the joint organizations and stimulate enterprise development.

The state, mandated by an Act, shall check the impediments to or restrictions of economic freedom and shall avoid or control any abuse that individuals or enterprises may create thanks to their dominant position in the national marketplace.

An Act shall delimit the scope of economic freedom when the social interest, the environment, and the cultural patrimony of the nation demand it." Oxford Constitutions (http://oxcon.ouplaw.com). © Oxford University Press, 2015. All Rights Reserved. Subscriber: Harvard University Library; date: 26 December 2016.

18 Article 58: "Private property and the other rights acquired in accordance with civil laws are guaranteed and may neither be disregarded nor infringed by subsequent laws. When in the application of a law enacted for reasons of public utility or social interest a conflict between the rights of individuals and the interests recognized by the law arises, the private interest shall yield to the public or social interest.

Property has a social dimension which implies obligations. As such, an ecological dimension is inherent to it.

The State shall protect and promote associative and joint forms of property.

Expropriation may be carried out for reasons of public utility or social interest defined by the legislator, subject to a judicial decision and prior compensation. The compensation shall be determined by taking into account the interests of the community and of the individual concerned. In the cases determined by the legislator, the expropriation may take place by administrative action, subject to subsequent litigation before the administrative law courts, including with regard to the price." Oxford Constitutions (http://oxcon.ouplaw.com). © Oxford University Press, 2015. All Rights Reserved. Subscriber: Harvard University Library; date: 26 December 2016.

19 Constitution of the Republic of Colombia, Chapter II, Of Social Economic Rights, Articles 42–79 in Oxford Constitutions (http://oxcon.ouplaw.com). © Oxford University Press, 2015. All Rights Reserved. Subscriber: Harvard University Library; date: 26 December 2016.

20 Constitution of the Plurinational State of Bolivia, Preamble.

21 For example, the charter specifically states in its Article 313 that the aim of the Bolivian economy is to eliminate poverty: "To eliminate poverty and social and economic exclusion, and in order to achieve the ideal of the good life in its multiple dimensions, the economic organization of Bolivia has the following goals." Oxford Constitutions (http://oxcon.ouplaw.com). © Oxford University

Press, 2015. All Rights Reserved. Subscriber: Harvard University Library; date: 26 December 2016.

22 Article 318 establishes these duties in the following terms: "**I.** The State shall determine a policy for the industrial and commercial production which guarantees a sufficient supply of goods and services to cover the basic domestic needs in an adequate manner and to strengthen the export capacity. **II.** The State recognizes and shall give priority to the support of associations of small and medium urban and rural businesses. **III.** The State shall strengthen the productive, manufacturing and industrial infrastructure and the basic services for the productive sector. **IV.** The State shall give priority to the promotion of rural productive development as the basis of the development policies of the country. **V.** The State shall promote and support the export of value added goods and services." Constitution of the Pluri-state of Bolivia in Oxford Constitutions (http://oxcon.ouplaw.com). © Oxford University Press, 2015. All Rights Reserved. Subscriber: Harvard University Library; date: 26 December 2016.

23 Article 320 directly states this privilege: "**I.** Bolivian investment shall be given priority over foreign investment."

24 Article 306 of the Constitution of the Pluri-state of Bolivia, in Oxford Constitutions (http://oxcon.ouplaw.com). © Oxford University Press, 2015. All Rights Reserved. Subscriber: Harvard University Library; date: 26 December 2016.

25 Article 320 – part **V.** "Public policies shall promote the internal consumption of products made in Bolivia."

26 Article 320 of the Pluri-National Constitution of Bolivia.

27 Article 56 of the Constitution of the Plurinational State of Bolivia.

28 Article 394 of the Constitution of the Plurinational State of Bolivia.

29 Article 57 the Constitution of the Plurinational State of Bolivia.

30 Article 56 of the Constitution of the Plurinational State of Bolivia.

31 An expansion of the ideas presented in this section can be found in Helena Alviar, "Neoliberalism as a Form of Authoritarian Constitutionalism," in *Authoritarian Constitutionalism: Comparative Analysis and Critique*, ed. Helena Alviar and Günter Frankenberg (Cheltenham: Edward Elgar, 2020), 37–56; Helena Alviar, "The Legal Architecture of Populism: Exploring Antagonists in Venezuela And Colombia," in *Human Rights in a Time of Populism: Challenges and Responses*, ed. Gerald E. Neuman (Cambridge: Cambridge University Press, 2020), 81–99.

32 For a more detailed analysis of this debate, see Helena Alviar, "Distribution of Resources Led by Courts: A Few Words of Caution," in *Social and Economic Rights in Theory and Practice: Critical Inquiries*, ed. Helena Alviar, Karl Klare and Lucy Williams (Abingdon: Routledge, 2015), 67–84.

33 Legislative act 3 of 2011, Article 1.

34 Ibid.

35 Ibid.

36 This style of governance is clearly described in the following terms: "A neoliberal governmentality is rooted in entrepreneurial values such as competitiveness, self-interest, and decentralization. It celebrates individual empowerment and the devolution of central state power to smaller localized units. Such a neoliberal mode of governance adopts the self-regulating free market as *the* model for proper government. Rather than operating along more traditional lines of pursuing the public good (rather than profits) by enhancing civil society and social justice, neoliberals call for the employment of governmental technologies

that are taken from the world of business and commerce: mandatory development of 'strategic plans' and 'risk-management' schemes oriented toward the creation of 'surpluses'; cost–benefit analyses and other efficiency calculations; the shrinking of political governance (so-called 'best-practice governance'); the setting of quantitative targets; the close monitoring of outcomes; the creation of highly individualized, performance-based work plans; and the introduction of 'rational choice' models that internalize and thus normalize market-oriented behaviour.

Neoliberal modes of governance encourage the transformation of bureaucratic mentalities into entrepreneurial identities where government workers see themselves no longer as public servants and guardians of a qualitatively defined 'public good' but as self-interested actors responsible to the market and contributing to the monetary success of slimmed-down state 'enterprises.'" Manfred B. Steger and Ravi K. Roy, *Neoliberalism: A Very Short Introduction* (Oxford: Oxford University Press, 2010).

37 There are many examples of this form of governance. A few of them would be the following. The Colombian Constitutional Court established in orders 185 of 2004, 178 of 2005, 218 of 2006 and 266 of 2006, that the absence of indexes to evaluate policies leading to overcome forced internal displacement in the country, was one of the prevalent obstacles, and consequently ordered the government to adopt impact indicators. (See Colombian Constitutional Court, Auto 185 of 2004, Auto 178 of 2005, Auto 218 of 2006, and Auto 266 of 2006). In the same way, the Department of National Planning presents the results of the national policies of rural development in terms of result indicators. These include indexes on land adjudication, social housing subsidies and farming credits granted, among others. (See Departamento de Planeación Nacional Colombia, "Desarrollo Rural Sostenible, Indicadores de Resultados de Política Pública," www.dnp.gov.co/programas/agricultura/estadisticas-del-sector-agropecuario/Paginas/Resultados-de-Pol%C3%ADtica-P%C3%BAblica.aspx (last consulted January 21, 2018.) And Article 1 of the National Development Plan 2014–2018, law 1753 of 2015, establishes that "the National Development Plan (. . .) has as an objective to build a Colombia in peace, equitable and educated, in harmony with the National Government's goals, in accordance with the best practices and international standards, and with the vision of long term planning foreseen in the objectives of sustainable development"; Article 20, in regard to the establishment of reserve areas for mining development, establishes "The Ministry of mines and energy will define strategic zones for mining-energetic development in no more than twelve (12) months from the date of issues of the present law. These zones will be declared for a term of two (2) years, extendable for the same period, and their objective is to allow for the organized management of the natural non-renewable resources, tending for the maximization of the use of the resources and adjusting to the best internationally accepted practices" (Colombia, Congreso de la República, Ley 1753 de 2015); Law 1715 of 2014, which regulates the integration of nonconventional renewable energies into the national energetic system states in Article 10, that the projects that are financed with the fund "will have to comply with cost-benefit evaluations that compare the costs of the project, with the projected savings or income produced" (Colombia, Congreso de la República, Ley 1715 de 2014); The Colombian Institute for Family Well-Being (ICBF) issued in 2009, a document titled "Best environmental practices for Community Homes of the Institute for Family Well-Being" (ICBF, "Mejores Prácticas Ambientales para

Hogares Comunitarios de Bienestar Familiar," www.superfinanciera.gov.co/ SFCant/Codigopais/textos/codigopias.pdf – last checked January 21, 2018).

38 For more on this analysis, see Helena Alviar, "The Legal Architecture of Populism: Exploring Antagonists in Venezuela and Colombia," in *Human Rights in a Time of Populism: Challenges and Responses*, ed. Gerald E. Neuman (Cambridge: Cambridge University Press, 2020), 81–99.

Bibliography

Agencia Bolivariana de Noticias. "Chávez: El que vote por el No lo hace por George W. Bush." *Aporrea*, November 30, 2007. www.aporrea.org/actualidad/n105636. html.

Alfonzo Paradisi, Juan Domingo. "Decretos Leyes Dictados en 2008 conforme a la Ley Habilitante de 2007 y su relación con la reforma constitucional improbada el 2 de diciembre de 2007." *Revista de Derecho Público, Ulpiano-Academia de Ciencias Políticas y Sociales* (2011): 98–105.

Alviar, Helena. "Distribution of Resources Led by Courts: A Few Words of Caution." In *Social and Economic Rights in Theory and Practice: Critical Inquiries*, edited by Helena Alviar, Karl Klare and Lucy Williams, 67–84. Abingdon: Routledge, 2015.

Alviar, Helena. "La búsqueda del progreso en la interpretación de la Constitución de 1991: El caso de la intervención de la Corte en la economía." In *Hacia un nuevo Derecho Constitucional*, edited by Daniel Bonilla and Manuel Iturralde. Bogotá: Uniandes, 2005.

Alviar, Helena. "Neoliberalism as a Form of Authoritarian Constitutionalism." In *In Authoritarian Constitutionalism: Comparative Analysis and Critique*, edited by Helena Alviar and Günter Frankenberg, 37–56. Cheltenham: Edward Elgar, 2020.

Alviar, Helena. "The Legal Architecture of Populism: Exploring Antagonists In Venezuela And Colombia." In *Human Rights In A Time of Populism: Challenges and Responses*, edited by Gerald E. Neuman, 81–99. Cambridge: Cambridge University Press, 2020.

Arias Castillo, Tomas A. "A manera de reflexión final: las cuatro delegaciones legislativas hechas al Presidente de la República (1999–2012)." *Revista de Derecho Público Ulpiano-Academia de Ciencias Políticas y Sociales*, no. 130 (2012): 393–99.

Armas, Mayela. "Modelo socialista se estructuró con leyes habilitantes." *El Universal*, December 2, 2013. www.venezuelaawareness.com/2013/12/ modelo-socialista-se-estructuro-con-leyes-habilitantes/.

Arze, Carlos, and Tom Kruse. "The Consequences of Neoliberal Reform." *NACLA Report on the Americas* 38, no. 3 (2004): 23–28.

Canon, Barry. *Hugo Chávez and the Bolivarian Revolution: Populism and democracy in a globalised age*. Manchester: Manchester University Press, 2010.

Cypher, James M., and James L. Dietz. *The Process of Economic Development*. London: Routledge, 2004.

Davis, Dennis M., and Karl Klare. "Transformative Constitutionalism and the Common and Customary Law." *South African Journal on Human Rights* 26, no. 3 (2010): 403–509.

de la Barra, Ximena, and Richard A. Dello Buono. *Latin America after the Neoliberal Debacle. Another Region Is Possible.* Lanham, MD: Rowman & Littlefield Publishers, 2009.

De Sousa Santos, Boaventura. *Refundación del Estado en América Latina.* Bogotá: Siglo del Hombre Editores, 2010.

Econométrica. "Maduro ha gobernado 53 meses con habilitantes y decretos de emergencia." *Econométrica*, February 7, 2018. www.econometrica.com.ve/blog/maduro-ha-gobernado-53-meses-con-habilitantes-y-decretos-de-emergencia/.

Frankenberg, Günter. *Comparative Constitutional Studies: Between Magic and Deceit.* Frankfurt: Edward Elgar, 2019.

Gargarella, Roberto. "Towards a Typology of Latin American Constitutionalism, 1810–60." *Latin American Research Review* 39, no. 2 (2004): 141–53.

Goldstein, Daniel M. "Decolonising 'Actually Existing Neoliberalism.'" *Social Anthropology* 20, no. 3 (2012): 304–9.

González Cadenas, Diego. *Un proceso constituyente democrático en Venezuela.* Bogotá: Uniandes, 2020.

Kohl, Benjamin H., and Linda C. Farthing. *Impasse in Bolivia: Neoliberal Hegemony and Popular Resistance.* London: Zed Books, 2006.

Krauss, Clifford. "New President in Venezuela Proposes to Rewrite the Constitution." *The New York Times*, February 4, 1999. www.nytimes.com/1999/02/04/world/new-president-in-venezuela-proposes-to-rewrite-the-constitution.html.

Krauze, Enrique. "Hell of a Fiesta." *The New York Review of Books*, March 8, 2018. www.nybooks.com/articles/2018/03/08/venezuela-hell-fiesta/.

Kushner, Rachel. *Telex from Cuba.* New York: Scribner, 2008.

Lee, Rebecca L. "Putting a Face on Free Market Economics: The Politicisation of Race and Ethnicity in Peru." *Race & Class* 51, no. 3 (2010): 47–58.

Lucero, José Antonio. "Decades Lost and Won: Indigenous Movements and Multicultural Neoliberalism in the Andes." In *Beyond Neoliberalism in Latin America? Societies and Politics at the Crossroads*, edited by John Burdick, Philip Oxhorn and Kenneth M. Roberts, 63–81. New York: Palgrave Macmillan, 2009.

May, James R., and Erin Daly. "Global Constitutional Environmental Rights." In *Routledge Handbook of International Environmental Law*, edited by Shawkat Alam, Jahid Hossain Bhuiyan, Tarew Chowdhury and Erika J. Techera, 605. London: Routledge, 2013.

McGee, Douglas A., and Kwanok Kim. "Constitutions, Economic Policy, And Citizen Support For Democratic Institutions: Peru And The Philippines In Comparative Perspective." *Pacific Focus* 12, no. 2 (2008): 111–38.

McGowan, Charis. "Chile Protests: What Prompted the Unrest?" *Al Jazeera*, October 30, 2019. Accessed 2020. www.aljazeera.com/news/2019/10/30/chile-protests-what-prompted-the-unrest/.

Oxford University Press. *Oxford Constitutions of the World,* 2015. https://oxcon.ouplaw.com/home/OCW.

Perreault, Thomas. "Extracting Justice: Natural Gas, Indigenous Mobilization, and the Bolivian State." In *The Politics of Resource Extraction. International Political Economy Series*, edited by Suzana Sawyer and Edmund T. Gomez, 75–102. London: Palgrave Macmillan, 2012.

PNUD. *Desiguales. Orígenes, cambios y desafíos de la brecha social en Chile.* Santiago de Chile: Programa de las Naciones Unidas para el Desarrollo, 2017.

Postero, Nancy. *Now We Are Citizens: Indigenous Politics in Postmulticultural Bolivia.* Stanford: Stanford University Press, 2006.

Postero, Nancy. "The Struggle to Create a Radical Democracy in Bolivia." *Latin American Research Review* 45 (2010): 59–78.

Ramirez, Carlos. "El crímen con las leyes habilitantes." *El Nacional*, November 30, 2017. www.elnacional.com/opinion/columnista/crimen-con-las-leyes-habilitantes_213483/.

Romero, Simon. "Venezuela Hands Narrow Defeat to Chávez Plan." *The New York Times*, December 3, 2007. www.nytimes.com/2007/12/03/world/americas/03venezuela.html.

Steger, Manfred B., and Ravi K. Roy. *Neoliberalism: A Very Short Introduction.* Oxford: Oxford University Press, 2010.

Taub, Amanda. " 'Chile Woke Up': Dictatorship's Legacy of Inequality Triggers Mass Protests." *The New York Times*, November 3, 2019. Accessed 2020. www.nytimes.com/2019/11/03/world/americas/chile-protests.html.

Tsolakis, Andreas. "Post-neoliberalism in Latin America?" In *Neoliberalism in Crisis*, edited by Henk Overbeek and Bastiaan van Apeldoorn, 187–89. New York: Palgrave Macmillan, 2012.

Uprimny, Rodrigo. "Las transformaciones constitucionales recientes en América Latina: tendencias y desafíos." In *El derecho en América Latina. Un mapa para el pensamiento jurídico del siglo XXI*, edited by César Rodríguez Garavito, 109–39. Bogotá: Siglo XXI Editores, 2011.

2 Providing access to property

Framed by economic development

The issue of land accumulation has been present in political, economic and legal debates in Latin America since independence. Notwithstanding diverse constitutional and legal transformations, framed within diverse theoretical approaches, unequal distribution of agrarian property continues to characterize most of the region and is central to economic development models.

Pedro Páramo, Juan Rulfo's short novel about the power of a big landowner, provides an insightful starting point for the prevalence of unequal access to property in the region. It depicts the deep consequences that resource concentration (in the form of big land extensions) has upon the lives of peasants beyond any data. Rulfo does this by exploring the figure of a despot, in Spanish *el terrateniente*, and how he manages to accumulate land by bending the law, using marriage and women's subordination, even controlling the forgiveness of god by dominating the town priest. The novel describes – in a direct and poetic way – the social, cultural and individual consequences that the concentration of power and resources in a landowner entail. Pedro Páramo decides on the life and death of the inhabitants of Comala; dispossesses and displaces peasants; mistreats women without any legal consequence. It is also a novel about a young man's coming of age journey and return to an ideal place only to find that it is desolate and barren. In sum, Rulfo is arguing that social, economic and political modernization (which includes the rule of law and the separation of powers) do not reach some rural areas of Latin America. After reading the novel, it is clear that the promises of the Mexican Revolution were empty promises in the countryside.

In a scene where Pedro and his administrator Fulgor Sedano are discussing the limits on his *latifundio*, the Media Luna, the following exchange occurs:

> He knocked with his whip handle at the door of Pedro Paramo's house, and thought of the first time he had knocked there two weeks earlier. He

waited a good while, just as he had waited the first time. He also saw once again the piece of black cloth that hung over the door. . . .

"Sit down, Fulgor. We can talk out here without being interrupted." They were in the back yard. Pedro Paramo sprawled out on a box and waited. "Why don't you sit down?"

"I'd rather stand up, Pedro."

"As you like. But don't forget the 'Don.'"

Who was this boy to speak to him like that? His father, Don Lucas Paramo had never insulted him like that, and here was this Pedro who hardly knew anything about the Media Luna or how it was run, treating him like a farm hand.

"How are things going?"

He felt his opportunity had arrived. "Now it's my turn," he said to himself.

"Worse and worse. There isn't anything left. We've sold the last animal. . . ."

"Who do we owe it to, I don't care how much, just who."

He read off a list of names. . . .

"Tomorrow we'll start to work. The Preciados first. Didn't you say we owe them the most?"

"Yes. And we've paid them the least. . . ."

"Tomorrow you're going to propose to Lola."

"She wouldn't even look at me, I'm too old."

"Propose for me. Tell her I'm very much in love with her. And while you're at it, tell Father Renteria to arrange for the wedding. . . ."

"The next thing is Alderete. Tell him he went beyond the boundaries. He's invaded lands that belong to the Media Luna."

"But he measured carefully. I think he is right."

"Tell him he made a mistake, he didn't measure correctly. Knock the fences down if you have to."

"And the law?"

"What law, Fulgor? From now on we're going to make the laws ourselves. Do you have any good tough men in the Media Luna?"

(Rulfo 1990)

Many central themes of this chapter can be fleshed out of this short quote. Fulgor, the farm administrator is now working for young Pedro right after his father has died. Being the owner gives him the status to demand he be called Don Pedro, despite his age and lack of experience. The logic of accumulation is central to the power of the landowner and he uses marriage to achieve it. Later on, the novel explores the link between property and patriarchy by describing sexual exploitation of women and Pedro's negligence toward his progeny. In addition, the excerpt illustrates how the *terrateniente* is above the law: "What law, Fulgor? From now on we're going to make the laws ourselves." This contempt paves the way for replacing the rule of law with the authoritarian, almost absolute power of the landowner.

Counteracting or promoting this style of power concentration has been essential to the history of property legislation in the region. This chapter hones into the different theoretical approaches that have influenced the way in which Latin American nations have used law to avoid property accumulation and dealt with demands for redistribution. It argues that the constitutional enshrinement of its social function; state ownership or formalization only regulate one aspect of property, and as a consequence limit its redistribution. As examples from different countries will illuminate, there are many additional factors determining access to property or the placing of limits over its concentration. Among them, the interaction with economic development goals; existing trade relations; the coexistence of multiple definitions of property and how to access it; the distribution of public spending on export led growth or import substitution industrialization; local and international demands of sustainable development; the rights of corporations and/ or foreign investors, as well as the commitment to collective property.

Throughout the twentieth century, most countries in the region set forth land reforms that, with varying degrees of strength, required a redefinition of property not as an individual, absolute right but as a social function that entails responsibilities. Because these reforms were so prevalent, the first part of the chapter analyzes the style of transformations that took a more centrist approach to the social function and those that enacted a more leftist, progressive one. These progressive reforms were inspired by Dependency Theory that advocated a major redistribution of resources from individuals to the nation state.

Then, it presents the neoliberal approach heralded by Hernando de Soto, which sees the market as the best resource distributor. From this perspective, the problem faced by Latin American countries in relation to property is a lack of modern market institutions necessary for its adequate exchange, protection and as a form to guarantee access to credit. This theoretical approach sees the solution as the formalization of the classical individual right to property in urban and rural settings. Finally, the text analyzes collective property as a possible counterpoint to individual accumulation.

The social function of property: tempering absolute freedom

De-individualizing property rights in order to include ideas about social duties and responsibilities was inspired by a combination of the goals embedded in the Mexican revolution,[1] along with the Weimar and the Spanish Constitutions.

The social function was aimed at replacing a natural, individual, absolute definition of property. It gave meaning to the term: the land is for those who work it, *la tierra es del que la trabaja*, which is a critique of both hoarding plots simply waiting for their value to increase and of the feudal-type relations that characterized most of the region. In other words, the social function tilted the balance toward peasants who had worked the land but were not owners. As a consequence, the state should protect property only when it fulfilled its social function and could therefore be authorized to seize it when this obligation was not being accomplished.

In addition, the government needed to play a central role in redistributing and providing access to land for peasants. As a matter of fact, during the early twentieth century, almost every country experimented with diverse attempts at agrarian reform. A few examples are Mexico in 1917,[2] Peru in 1970,[3] Ecuador in 1979,[4] Colombia in 1968,[5] Venezuela in 1960,[6] Guatemala,[7] Honduras,[8] Nicaragua[9] and Cuba.[10] These reforms were very diverse in terms of their scope as well as in relation to the political and economic objectives they pursued, but all of them were inspired by the social function ideal.

The centrist approach – distribution led by the state for import substitution industrialization

Land reform was an integral component of import substitution industrialization (ISI),[11] a combination of policies set in place from the late 1950s through the mid 1980s in Latin America. Despite the fact that agriculture was secondary compared to the industrial, urban sector during the ISI era, agrarian reform played an important role. In fact, distributing land in the countryside was important in order to alleviate poverty, providing peasants with much needed resources to buy what was produced by the local industrial sector that was being protected. Not all rural property should be the object of redistribution, mostly barren land, frontier plots and a handful of large extensions that were not fulfilling what was defined as its social function (Alviar, The Unending Quest For Land: The Tale Of Broken Constitutional Promises 2011).

In addition, during the import substitution industrialization era, many countries in the region saw agrarian reform as a way to mechanize production and promote the migration of workers to cities in order for them to be employed in protected industries. In other cases, agrarian reform was seen as a way to get small plot owners to produce goods for export, where a labor force was hard to find, as in the case of coffee in Colombia (Palacios 1980)

(Alviar, Italian Coffee: Retelling the Story 2020). Later on, land reform fulfilled the somewhat paradoxical objective of avoiding migration from the rural areas to the cities when it became clear that there were not enough jobs provided by the policies of ISI.

Many countries in the region set in place these centrist types of reform, among them Colombia,[12] Ecuador,[13] Venezuela[14] and Costa Rica[15] during the late 1950s and 1960s; Honduras[16] and Peru[17] during the 1970s.[18] The most radical reforms were found in Cuba and Bolivia, where 80% of the arable land was redistributed. In Mexico, Chile, Peru and Nicaragua, almost half of the land was expropriated. In Colombia, Venezuela, Panama, El Salvador and the Dominican Republic, it was a little less than 25% (Teubal and Ortega Breña 2009).

An example of a centrist approach: Colombia

In 1936, the concept of social function of property was included for the first time in the constitution through an amendment. The reform was the product of several years of unrest that had acquired force since the early 1920s. Disputes over land property were at the heart of these struggles. At the time, many peasants who had tenant-type arrangements – contracts by which they would be allowed to use a piece of land in exchange for a price, either money, work or part of the harvest – were expelled from the land. This happened for two reasons; first, because landowners found it more efficient and in some cases cheaper to hire them as workers (Molina 1984) and second because as land was becoming more and more valuable, landowners saw a risk that the tenants would claim ownership to it (after 20 years of possession[19]). The eviction of independent laborers in the regions of highest land quality increased property concentration and at the same time fired social unrest.

The legal solution was provided by the incorporation of Leon Duguit's ideas of property rights limited by a social purpose. Among members of the ruling liberal party, there was a group that understood that they needed to transform their political message in order to try to put an end to the escalating social conflicts, and at the same time, get the votes of the workers and landless peasants. Once the progressive wing of the liberal party was in power, they needed to institutionalize this ideological shift by providing the necessary constitutional and legal instruments. As a consequence, the government presented a constitutional reform project whose objective was to "de-individualize" the concept of rights and to modernize the state in order to allow it to intervene in the economy and promote social change.[20]

Later that same year, law 200 was passed in order to develop the constitutional provision. This law established a property presumption in favor of those who occupied the land and were exploiting it economically.[21] It also included ownership in favor of squatters who in good faith thought that the land had no previous owner and the extinction of the right of ownership for rural property that was more than 300 hectares.[22] The legal provision had very meager results in terms of redistribution, for various reasons. On the one hand, landowners became more diligent in evicting squatters before they could acquire the land after occupying it for the legally required years, and there was no government effort to declare property extinction.

Almost 30 years later, given its meager results in terms of redistribution (and concerned with the specter and demands of the Cuban revolution) the government proposed a new agrarian reform. This reform reiterated the need to transform the rural structure of the country by eliminating unequal land concentration, promoting its productive and efficient use, distributing property to landless peasants, giving preference to those who directly work the land or were employed as such.[23] One of its guiding principles was to "[p]romote adequate economic exploitation and social use of rural lands."[24] It also created the Colombian Land Reform Institute (INCORA) in order to manage and distribute land that had no owner, frontier land of public domain. The Institute could also acquire private lands in order to comply with the law objectives.[25]

The 1961 reform faced several obstacles.[26] First, the impulse to redistribute land found very strong political resistance. Instead of breaking up excessive property accumulation, a great amount of the granted plots were in frontier lands, not suitable for agriculture with little or no access to water or roads given their remote location. INCORA acquired land to distribute during its first three years of existence and then the acquisition process was halted. All throughout, distribution was inefficient (R. Findley 1972).

Furthermore, after the late 1950s the economic development model set in place in Colombia was almost completely geared toward industrialization through the import substitution industrialization model. This fact had at least two consequences. First, there was a lack of public resources geared toward setting in place land distribution and instead most of state spending was dedicated to an improvement in industrial productivity (R. Findley 1972) and little attention was paid to the needs of agricultural development.

Finally, the judicial branch also contributed to the legal rigidities that prevented the constitutional promise from crystallizing. This happened basically in two ways. The first one was the combination of administrative and judicial instances that prolonged adjudication processes and made distribution uncertain. On the other hand, the Council of State (judicial instance for administrative decisions) developed a legal position that required a second visit for contested expropriated land. This fact gave the property owners the opportunity to make the necessary adjustments in order to prove the productive use of land (R. Findley 1972). The 1991 Constitution went further than the 1936 reform. In fact, Article 58 of the 1991 document adopted the wording of Article 30 of the previous constitution, added an ecological function and established the possibility to expropriate without compensation if public interest matters were at stake.[27] The ecological function was defined by the Constitutional Court as the prohibition to indiscriminately exploit natural resources and effective limits over private property.[28] These limits over private property were reiterated in several Constitutional Court rulings. One of the most relevant was a decision in 1993 that linked the distribution of land to democracy.[29] Nevertheless, the social function was weakened through a 1999 constitutional reform that eliminated expropriation without compensation. This amendment was proposed by the government as a way to feign off fears of foreign investors. In addition, and according to debate documents, this expropriation ran counter to several bilateral investment treaties of which Colombia was a party, and the provisions of the American Convention on Human Rights on expropriation with just compensation.[30]

Ambitious redistribution: dependency inspired reforms

Dependency Theory influenced agrarian reform impulses in other countries of Latin America. This section analyzes the case of Cuba because it provides a showcase of this theory, and of its shortcomings as well.

The overarching objectives of agrarian reforms in leftist governments were directed toward eliminating wealth concentration and promoting an economic development model that is defined, planned, controlled and managed by state institutions. As will become evident in this section, Dependency inspired reforms are exactly the opposite of what was described in the previous section regarding the centrist social function of property. Key differences include a shift in the importance of private property, the redistribution of enormous swaths of land, the speed with which laws and administrative regulations were set forth and the number of beneficiaries.

In the cases of Cuba (Peñalver 2000), Nicaragua (Stanfield and Hendrix 1993) and, more recently, Venezuela (Ankersen and Ruppert 2006), the land that was redistributed was most of the productive soil of a nation. In addition, private property was not considered one of the basic individual rights that defines a citizen. Rather, public or national property was essential and, in the cases of Cuba and Nicaragua at least, agriculture was central to state-led economic development.

Cuba

Since its Constitution of 1940, private property in Cuba was framed within the limits of social purpose and public interest.[31] At the time of the revolution, Cuba's most important economic sector was agriculture. Therefore, as would be expected, one of the first laws passed by the government of Fidel Castro was an agrarian reform law (Hendrix 1996).[32] The property that was immediately confiscated was that belonging to people or corporations found responsible for crimes against the Cuban economy or the national treasury that had been committed during the Batista dictatorship. These included the property of Batista and his cooperators (Hendrix 1996); the property of those engaged in criminal activities, who were enriched unfairly or illegally as a consequence of it; assets that belonged to counterrevolutionaries as well as abandoned property (Hendrix 1996). In addition, the government took control over banks, public utilities and other necessary areas of production.

By 1961, more than 40% of private property had been expropriated, close to four million hectares of the most fertile land (Hendrix 1996). Large estates were forbidden and limits were placed over the maximum amount a person could own. Anything above this limit could be expropriated and later redistributed. The only exceptions that allowed for bigger land concentration were productive sugar cane plantations, cattle farming meeting the minimum standards set by the Agrarian Reform Institute and highly productive rice plantations. Land that was unproductive two years after the agrarian reform law would be subject to expropriation (Hendrix 1996). The law also stated the amount of land foreigners were allowed to own (Hendrix 1996).[33] Along with the goal to end the unequal distribution of wealth, the idea was also to become self-sufficient in food production and to achieve full employment in one generation. In Fidel Castro's own words:

> I ask the people, if they agree or disagree with the fact that our revolutionary government is organizing cooperatives so that peasants don't have to pay double for goods; I ask the people if they agree or not that they have were to work. [. . .]
>   If they disagree with our goal to repopulate the Cuban countryside which was desolate as a result of the selfishness and ambition of big landowners. [. . .]
>   If they agree or not with us harvesting our own rice instead of importing it; the oil we need without importing it, the cotton we need without importing it; the food we need without importing it, in order to give a job to more than a million Cubans who have no job. I as the people if they disagree with our industrialization plans.
>
> (Castro 1959)

Later on, the first Revolutionary Constitution of 1976 established that Cuba was a socialist state of workers, peasants and other manual and intellectual workers.[34] It included state ownership of the means of production and determined that all property belonged to the nation except for that owned by small producers and cooperatives. Small owners could form cooperatives in order to get certain public services, such as technical assistance and access to pesticides or equipment. They could also sell their land, provided that the state approved of it. Renting, sharecropping and mortgage credit were constitutionally forbidden, and land could only be inherited by those who worked on it.[35] Expropriation was enshrined, and it included a compensation of a bit less than fair market value.[36]

In the following 15 years, there were a few changes: the advancement in the expropriation of large estates;[37] the reduction of the maximum landholdings per person, along with the expropriation of all farms above this size. This ended the exception allowing large farms for sugar cane and rice among other products.

Despite Castro's plans to industrialize, these attempts were short lived. Cuba was centered around the export of sugar cane during the first 30 years of the revolution. Initially, the Castro government had as its goal to reach the production of ten million tons of sugar by 1970.[38] In order to reach this objective, Cuba had to move from supporting small farmers to a planned, modern agro-industrial sector. Public resources were given mostly to state-owned farms and land-labor cooperatives. Exports were directed to markets where Cuban sugar had preferential treatment in the Soviet-led Council of Mutual Economic Assistance – COMECON.[39]

The 1990s proved to be a very difficult period for the Cuban economy, once COMECON was dismantled between 1989 and 1991. As a consequence, the country faced shortages of machinery, diesel as well as repair parts for tractors, harvesters and processing plants. Production of sugar decreased by 50% (Thiemann and Spoor 2019). The crisis was strongly felt, and between 1989 and 1994 malnutrition was widespread. In what could be called a counter-agrarian reform and in order to respond to the crisis, the Castro government created incentives for the production of food in or around cities through a land reform that granted small plots of urban and semi-urban land to individuals, allowing these small producers to sell their goods at market prices (Thiemann and Spoor 2019). Peasant-owned farms and cooperatives became essential for food production in the country, and by 2006 they represented 65% of domestic food production (Thiemann and Spoor 2019). Along with this revitalization of small and subsistence farmers, most of the land dedicated to sugar cane and other export crops abandoned during the late 1980s was left unused. In 2008, Raul Castro embarked on yet another land reform in an effort to create incentives for individuals and their families to take over abandoned land and make it productive.[40]

Coming back to the individual and strengthening the market: neoliberal reforms

Background

As will be discussed throughout this book, neoliberalism has many dimensions to it. Far from being a uniform, coherent theory, certain aspects of it are strengthened and others are weakened depending on the area of the economy where it is being applied, along with the geographical and geopolitical context of specific countries and their existing institutions.

Neoliberal ideas about agriculture in Latin America start out by recentering the importance of this sector for export-led growth and comparative advantage. This renewed emphasis on the world division of production shed a different light on the rural sector. Countries in the region with vast, productive and underused lands (in and near the Amazon, for example) became the focus of legal reforms to promote property formalization. In addition, economic development goals promoting agrobusiness allowed big landowners to influence policy design. In Colombia, for example, the palm oil industry received a significant allocation of government resources through the Rural Capital Incentive (ICR). That assistance was also accompanied by tax exemptions and favored large- and medium-scale growers (Potter 2015). In Peru, government incentives for growing palm oil included tax exemptions, and the goal of many regulations – after the ratification of the Free Trade Agreement in 2007 – was to create a land market in the Amazon in order to establish biofuel crops, as well as mining and oil exploration on indigenous lands (Potter 2015).

Neoliberalism is also a critique of both neoclassical interventionist and dependency agrarian policies. These critiques were related to the social confrontation between landowners and peasants, which paralyzed redistributive efforts; excessive state intervention in the market, which overpriced plots and arbitrarily allocated property; and the lack of an integral policy that should always include plans for efficient productivity and adequate commercialization programs (Alviar, The Unending Quest for Land: The Tale of Broken Constitutional Promises 2011).

This individualist, liberal perspective on land reform opposes property accumulation because of the inefficient use of big land extensions. Nevertheless, the way to solve this problem is not through state intervention to redistribute unproductive or frontier land, rather the idea is to create the conditions for land to be bought and sold according to market prices. In order for the market to function, titling is essential to know who owns what. Along with knowing who owns what, the mechanism to improve access to land is to provide credit to landless peasants (instead of receiving property through state-run agrarian reform institutes). Credit should only be granted when recipients have proved they need the land in order to advance a feasible productive project.[41] The plan went beyond formalizing property rights, of course. Both governments and multilateral institutions, such as the World Bank, imagined a road out of poverty paved by creating property owners. If individuals had titles, they could use their land or homes as collateral for loans. The loans in turn would provide the seed for small businesses that would in turn increase the value of property.

In addition to boosting ideas about comparative advantage and export-led growth, the shift from the state to the market and the emphasis of the individual versus the collective, neoliberal reforms in the region included the aim of a balanced budget, which was set forth through steep cuts in public spending. As a consequence, agricultural subventions were reduced, subsidized credit was eliminated and investment in technical support or local scientific research was dismantled. Foreign investment was allowed to enter freely into the rural sector, which in turn transformed agriculture and in many cases privileged the harvesting of biofuels over food production (Yohannes 2018).

Peru

Perú is a very telling example of neoliberal policies set forth early on and in a forceful and comprehensive way, which included scaling back on indigenous collective rights and promoting property accumulation for the purpose of advancing agrobusiness projects.

These reforms were greatly influenced by Peruvian economist Hernando de Soto, who argued that strong and clear property rights would encourage investment and in turn generate economic development. De Soto advanced his ideas against the backdrop of accusations regarding the profound inequality that characterized the country, made by the guerrilla group *Sendero Luminoso* (Shining Path). As a matter of fact, the name of his book is a direct reference to the group: *The Other Path: The Economic Answer to Terrorism* (De Soto 1989). As Timothy Mitchell aptly puts it, formalization was a way to both give access to property to the poor and provide a solution to inequality that would counterbalance the demands of the leftist guerrilla group:

> The populism of de Soto's neoliberal program, emphasizing the virtue of property rights for the poor, was intended as an answer to the more radical property redistribution programs of the revolutionaries – as well

as to the problems of large-scale urban migration caused by warfare in the countryside between the rebels and the Peruvian armed forces. The war against the Sendero Luminoso and its effects on one particular city shaped both the property rights experiment and the research experiment to which it gave rise.

(Mitchell 2015)

In 1991, the Fujimori government passed the Law for the Promotion of Investment in the Agrarian Sector (Legislative Decree 653 of 1991) in order to formalize individual property and provide secure transactions for investors in the Amazon. This law effectively ended the agrarian reform that had been set in place in the years before. A constitutional reform in 1993 modified communal property in order to allow communities to divide and sell their land, permitting foreign investment in these areas. The reform ended the "inalienable" character of indigenous titles.[42] Two years later, the Fujimori government expanded the possibilities for peasants and native communities to break collectively owned land by passing the Law of Private Investment in the Development of Economic Activities in the National Territory and of the Peasant and Native Communities Lands (Law 26505 of 1995). This law also promoted a shift toward agrobusiness by allowing both indigenous communities and peasants to select between being organized as a community or joining a stock company.[43] This emphasis on individual property rights was a direct attack on collective ones, which were seen as hindering economic development. In a BBC article published in 2010, Hernando de Soto explains why he was against collective property and why individual titling was the solution:

In Santa Ursula the Apu – the leader – carefully unfolds a photocopy of the community's land title. Attached is a map showing their demarcated territory.

It is a communal land title, issued according to the law that gave recognition to Native Communities in the Amazonian region.

But Hernando de Soto says this law has isolated them from the global economy.

"It doesn't make them part of the system. I'm sure the title was given to them with the best of intentions, but there are restrictions," he says.

"It's communal, they aren't recognized as private individuals.

"It's like a telephone that only connects to one other telephone, while your telephone connects to 6bn other telephones

[. . .]

"They need what the rest of us have – clear property rights over what they own, so that they can get credit and capital, and so that there's no discussion over who owns what.

"And the second thing they need is organization. You can do business with an organization; you can't do business with a tribe."

(BBC 2010)

Privileging individual titling and property accumulation as well as extractive industries and agrobusiness continues to be the rule in Peru 20 years after the Fujimori government passed the initial reforms. According to some research, 41.2% of the Peruvian Amazon is under oil or gas concessions (Monterroso et al. 2017).

Property formalization did not bring the transformation neoliberals promised in Peru. In his fascinating analysis of legal informality in the context of Panama City, Jorge Esquirol describes the questionable benefits of these measures:

> In Peru, where mass titling programs since 1996 have been widespread, "[access to mortgage loans by virtue of owning registered property has been negligible" and "there is no evidence that formalization is leading to the development of formal land markets among the low-income population." At the end of the day, these programs may not advance their own much vaunted goals. Instead, their only effect may be to consolidate a more rigid conception of private property rights. Furthermore, it is not clear that a monolithic slate of property rights is preferable in all cases to different modes of asset allocation. At a minimum, the overwhelming push for titled property rights limits possibilities for other alternatives.
>
> (Esquirol 2014)

Table 2.1 summarizes the three theoretical approaches described earlier.

Table 2.1 Summary of three theoretical approaches

	Definition	*Beneficiaries*	*Idea about Property*
Centrist	Redistribution to improve use of land and internal market	Poor, landless peasants	Social function, individual
Dependency Theory	Redistribution to transform classes system in society	Peasants, but potentially all citizens	Social function, public
Neoliberal Theory	Improve access and functioning of land market	Proven need and productive project	Individual property

Collective property: a true counterpoint?

During the late 1980s and 1990s, many Latin American countries included multicultural citizenship provisions that recognized the culturally mixed character of many societies. This included mentioning specific ethnic or racial groups as a foundational part of a nation; registering customary law as official public law; giving status for minority languages as well as guaranteeing bilingual education and, importantly for the purpose of this chapter, granting collective property rights to land.[44] Argentina, Bolivia, Brazil, Colombia, Costa Rica, Ecuador, Guatemala, Honduras, Mexico, Nicaragua, Panama, Paraguay, Peru and Venezuela all have constitutionally enshrined collective rights to property (Hooker 2005).

Collective property rights are deemed essential to achieve the autonomy that is promised to indigenous groups by effectively granting them jurisdiction over a specific area of land. Some countries protected this right in an uninterrupted form since colonial times and others established it later. Constitutional provisions that include the right to collective property also prohibit the selling or mortgaging of collective title and exclude them from paying taxes. Mexico weakened these prohibitions in 1993[45] and Peru did the same in 1995.[46] Brazilian indigenous groups have only the right of collective use, the property belongs to the federal government.[47] Most charters establish that the state owns the subsoil and although they must consult with indigenous communities about the exploitation of these resources, this has proved highly controversial in governments both to the left and to the right (Van Cott 2000).

Notwithstanding the fact that collective property provides a counterpoint to classical liberal understanding of property as well as the collectivization typical of socialism, many have argued that the granting of this type of arrangement in Latin America was more attuned with the neoliberal agenda[48] than with ideas of protecting mother earth or *Buen Vivir* defended in Bolivia and Ecuador. The reason for this being the marginal character of collective titling when compared with individual property rights, the slow pace at which this type of property has been granted and the constant reduction of decision capacity over their land that indigenous groups have.

Conclusions

The profound consequences that property accumulation has over a nation continue to be as relevant today as they were when Juan Rulfo wrote *Pedro Páramo* in the early twentieth century. The conditions in which it happens and the power it vests over the very few continue to be at the center of political, economic and social struggles in the region.

This chapter analyzed three different theoretical approaches to face the challenge of property accumulation. The ideological strands and goals dealing with land concentration, growth and social transformation are quite diverse. The ones included in this chapter were picked to illustrate archetypes of legal and economic development goals that influence property. They were not intended to provide full or detailed pictures of each country. As each description made evident, the three approaches outlined – the social, Dependency Theory and neoliberalism – are far from monolithic, determining unchangeable paths. Rather, all three of them have had to morph as a result of the demands from the global context, shifting local pressure or a combination of both.

In addition, the constitutional enshrinement of the social function of property, the ambitious redistribution through state ownership or the impulse to formalize only regulate the starting point of initial access. As the examples from different archetypes exemplified, there are additional components that determine how property is exercised and possibilities for its accumulation. These additional elements include the interaction with economic development goals; existing trade relations; the coexistence of individual and collective titling; levels of public spending on export led growth or import substitution industrialization; local and international environmental demands along with the rights of corporations and/or foreign investors.

Notes

1 "In Latin America, the Mexican Revolution coincided with this era and its 1917 constitution, discussed below, represents the world's first example of what has been called 'social constitutionalism.' Following Mexico, other states in Europe and Latin America explicitly incorporated the Duguitian idea of social function in their constitutions." T. Thomas Ankersen and Thomas Ruppert, "Tierra y Libertad: The Social Function Doctrine and Land Reform in Latin America," *Tulane Environmental Law Journal* (2006): 76.

2 Republic of Mexico, Federal Constitution, 1917, Article 27: "The property of the lands and waters within the limits of the national territory originally corresponds to the Nation, which has the right to transmit its domain to individuals, constituting private property. . . . The nation will have at all times the right to impose on private property the modalities dictated by the public interest, as well as to regulate, for social benefit, the use of natural elements capable of appropriation, in order to make an equitable distribution of public wealth." Transcription: "La propiedad de las tierras y aguas comprendidas dentro de los límites del territorio nacional, corresponde originariamente a la Nación, la cual ha tenido y tiene el derecho de transmitir el dominio de ellas a los particulares, constituyendo laA propiedad privada [. . .]. The nation will at all times have the right to impose on private property the modalities dictated by the public interest, as well as to regulate, for social benefit, the use of natural elements susceptible to appropriation, in order to make an equitable distribution of public wealth [. . .]."

3 Rural Reform Law, Law Decree No. 17716, 1970, Article 1: "The Rural Reform is an instrument of transformation of the agrarian structure of the country destined to substitute the regimes of latifundio and minifundio with a fair system of property, possession and exploitation of the land, that contributes to the social and economic development of the Nation." Article 3, literal a): "The Rural Reform must: Regulate the right to own land so that it is used in harmony with the social interest. Article 5: "It is of public utility and social interest the expropriation of rustic properties of private property in the conditions established by this law." Article 10: "The affectation consists of the limitation of the right of rural property imposed for the purposes of Agrarian Reform on all or part of a property for its expropriation by the State and its subsequent adjudication to peasants." It is interesting that Article 15 c) explicitly states specific circumstances in which rural property does not contribute to social interest: Article 15: "Private property is considered not to be used in harmony with social interest in the following cases: [. . .]. " The Constitution of Peru of 1933 also states the relationship between property and social function: Constitución Política del Perú de 1933: Article 34: "Property must be used in harmony with the social interest. The law shall establish the limits and modalities of the right to property."

4 Rural Reform Law, R.O. 877–18-VII, 1979. As well as the law in Peru, this law includes de concept of "afectación," which consists on the total or partial limitation of property rights on rustic lands that do not fulfill the social function. Also, this law also states the specific cases when rural property does not fulfill its social function. For further reading, see Maldonado Lince Guillermo, "La reforma agraria en el Ecuador," En: *Cahiers du monde hispanique et luso-brésilien*, n°34, 1980. Numéro consacré à l'Équateur. pp. 33–56.

5 Rural Reform Law, Law 1, 1968.

6 Rural Reform Law, G.O.611, 1960.

7 Guatemala, Rural Reform Law, Decree 900, 1952.

8 Rural Reform Law, D.O. 21–482, 1975.

9 Rural Reform Law, 1981.

10 Second Rural Reform Law, October 3, 1963.

11 "ISI was a development model set of public policies intended to promote industrialization in developing countries through state intervention. This protectionism is carried out through a range of policies which include the following: the incorporation of tariffs upon manufactured imports; the institution of credit programs and subsidies to promote the creation and strengthening of domestic industry; the creation of public institutions in charge of promoting industrial activities; the establishment of differential exchange rates for the import of capital goods; and, the establishment of state owned industries." Helena Alviar, "The Classroom and the Clinic: The Relationship between Clinical Legal Education, Economic Development and Social Transformation," *UCLA Journal of International Law and Foreign Affairs* 13, no. 1 (Spring 2008): 197–218.

12 Law 135, 1961; Law 1, 1968.

13 Rural Reform and Colonization Law, 1964.

14 Rural Reform Law, 1960.

15 Law 2825, 1961.

16 Law Decree 170, 1974.

17 Rural Reform Law, 1964, Law Decree 17716, 1970.

18 For a more complete description on agrarian reform typology, see Helena Alviar Garcia, *Desarrollo, Teoría Feminista y Derecho: Propuestas para un análisis distributivo* (Bogotá: Ediciones Uniandes-Editorial Temis, 2008).

19   Civil Code, Article 2531. The 20-year period required in this article to acquire property through possession was lowered to ten years by Article 2 of Law 791 of 2002.

20   For a more detailed analysis of this reform, see Helena Alviar Garcia, "Leon Duguit's Influence in Colombia: The Last Opportunity of a Potentially Progressive Reform," in *Order from Transfer: Comparative Constitutional Design and Legal Culture*, ed. Gunter Frankenberg (Cheltenham: Edgar Elgar, 2013), 306–21.

21   Economically exploiting the land meant according to the law: "positive acts of ownership, such as planting, occupation with cattle, and other acts of economic meaning." See Ley 200 de 1936, Article 1.

22   Law 200, 1936, Article 6: The extinction of the rights of ownership will have no effect in relation to the following properties: 1st. Those with a total capacity of less than three hundred (300) hectares that constitute the sole rural property of the respective owner [. . .] (translation by the author); Article 12: Establish an acquisitive prescription of the domain in favor of who, believing in good faith that it is wasteland, owns for five continuous years privately owned land not exploited by its owner (translation by the author).

23   Law 135, 1961, Article 1: To provide land to those who do not possess it, preferably to those who must directly conduct their exploitation and incorporate their personal work into it.

24   Law 135, 1961, Article 1, numeral 2.

25   Law 135, 1961, Article 2: The Colombian Institute of Agrarian Reform is created as a public establishment, that is, as an entity endowed with legal personality, administrative autonomy and its own heritage; Article 3, a): "Administer on behalf of the State the nationally owned wastelands"; Article 3, h): Carry out land acquisition programs in rural areas, through direct negotiation with the owners who voluntarily transfer them or decree their expropriation.

26   There are many articles that describe these frustrating results. Among them Karst L. Kenneth, "The Colombian Land Reform Law: 'The Contribution of an Independent Judiciary,'" *The American Journal of Comparative Law* (1965): 118–24: "Professor Hirschman reports that opponents on the political left and right had the votes to block a two-thirds vote. With this fact in mind, the passage of the bill was rushed to meet the December, 1961 deadline established in an earlier emergency measure, adopted after the overthrow of the Rojas Pinilla dictatorship, which purported to dispense with the two-thirds vote requirement in cases of 'social' legislation. The constitutionality of uncompensated takings of land then rests on a validation of the emergency provision which purported to suspend the two-thirds vote requirement, and on a characterization of the land reform law as 'social' legislation"; Roger Findley, *Ten Years of Land Reform in Colombia* (Madison, WI: Wisconsin Law Review, 1972); Peter Dorner and Herman Felstehausen, "Agrarian Reform and Employment: The Columbian Case," *International Labour Review* (1970): 21–240; T. Thomas Ankersen and Thomas Ruppert, "Tierra y Libertad: The Social Function Doctrine and Land Reform in Latin America," *Tulane Environmental Law Journal* (2006): 12–76; Joseph R. Thome, "Limitaciones de la Legislación Colombiana para Expropiar o Comprar Fincas con Destino de Parcelación," *Interamerican Law Review* (1996): 281–91.

27   For more on the ecological function and the 1991 reform, see Helena Alviar, "Looking Beyond the Constitution: The Social and Ecological Function of

Property," in *Comparative Constitutional Law in Latin America,* ed. Rosalind Dixon and Tom Ginsburg (Cheltenham: Edgar Elgar, 2017).

28 The Court in 2006 stated this limit in the following terms: "As this Court has said before, the establishment of the ecological function situates the environment as a limit to the exercise of private property." Colombian Constitutional Court, Ruling C-189 of 2006, M.P. Rodrigo Escobar Gil.

29 Decision C-006 of 1993, per Justice Eduardo Cifuentes Muñoz: "The numerous constitutional provisions on access to property as inscribed in a frameset of distributive justice and seek to give a real basis to the principles of participative democracy and equality of opportunities. Democracy with hunger is a utopia and a farce. The unequal distribution of income and goods is only compatible with a declaration of rights but not with their full and unrestricted exercise. Thus, along with the previously affirmed dimension of adequate exploitation of property traditionally associated with the social function of property, there is now an idea of equality which must be placed in equal footing. Equality is not only the condition for legitimacy of private property, but also the justification for emancipatory processes in favor of an overwhelming number of landless people."

30 Congress gazette No. 189 de 1999, 21 September 1998, p. 2: "We consider it of the utmost importance to submit to the consideration of the Honorable Congress of the Republic a draft legislative act that modifies Article 58 of the Charter, in the sense of allowing the National Government the possibility of concluding International Agreements in which it is agreed that any case expropriation will have fair and equitable compensation."); p. 5: "subsection 5 of article 58 of the National Constitution, which establishes expropriation without compensation on the basis of equity, constitutes a clear risk of expropriation without compensation for the investor, since the reasons for equity are not defined nor are there clear and precise criteria to assess the extent of expropriation for equity reasons."

31 Cuban Constitution, 1940, Article 87: "The Cuban State recognizes the existence and legitimacy of private property in its broadest concept of social function and without more limitations than those established by law for reasons of public necessity or social interest" (translation by me).

32 Steven E. Hendrix, "Tensions in Cuban Property Law," *Hastings International and Comparative Law Review* (1996): 16–39.

33 Ibid., 11.

34 Cuba's Constitution of 1976, Article 1: "The Republic of Cuba is a socialist State of workers and peasants and other manual workers and intellectual."

35 Cuban Constitution of 1976, Article 21: "Leasing, sharecropping, mortgage [. . .] are prohibited"; Article 24: "The land of small farmers is only inheritable by those heirs who work it personally."

36 Cuba's Constitution of 1976, Article 25: "The expropriation of property is authorized. [. . .] The law establishes the procedure for expropriation [. . .] as well as the form of compensation."

37 Second Rural Reform Law, Hendrix, "Tensions in Cuban Property Law," 48.

38 Castro Launches 10 Million Ton Sugar Harvest, 1969, transcript, http://lanic.utexas.edu/project/castro/db/1969/19691028.html.

39 Soviet-led Council of Mutual Economic Assistance (COMECON) was an organization for economic development conformed by large preferential export markets. Louis Thiemann and Max Spoor, "Beyond the 'Special Period': Land

54   *Providing access to property*

Reform, Supermarkets and the Prospects for Peasant-Driven Food Sovereignty in Post-Socialist Cuba (2008–2017)," *Canadian Journal of Development Studies* (2019): 3, 548–50.
40 Law Decree 259 of 2008.
41 For more on this neoliberal style of reform, see Helena Alviar, "The Unending Quest For Land: The Tale, Broken Constitutional Promises," *Texas Law Review* (2011): 1895–914.
42 Unlike their previous Constitution of 1979, which in Article 161 stated that "The Peasant and Native Communities [. . .] are autonomous in their organization, their communal work and their use of the land," Article 89 of Peru's Constitution of 1993 allowed the free disposal of communal property: "The Peasant and Native Communities [. . .] are autonomous in their organization, in communal work and in the use and free disposal of their lands."
43 Article 8: "The Peasant Communities and the Native Communities are free to adopt, by majority agreement of their members, the business organization model they decide"; Article 9: "Peasant associative companies are free to contract and associate with any other company."
44 Colombian Constitution of 1991, Articles 7, 10, 63; Peruvian Constitution of 1993, Articles 2, 17, 88, 89, 149; Constitution of Ecuador of 1998, Articles 1, 83, 84, 85, 191, 224; Venezuelan Constitution of 1999, Articles 9, 119, 120, 121, 122, 123, 124, 125, 126; Mexican Constitution of 1917, Articles 2, 27.
45 Agrarian law, 1992, Article 75: "In cases of manifest utility for the nucleus of the ejido population, it may transmit the domain of common use lands to mercantile or civil societies in which the ejido or ejidatarios participate."
46 Law 26505, 1995, Article 11: "To dispose, lease or exercise any other act on the communal lands of the Sierra or Selva, the Agreement of the General Assembly will be required with the consent vote of not less than two thirds of all the members of the Community."
47 Constitution of Brazil of 1988, Article 231: "The social organization, customs, languages, creeds and traditions of Indians are recognized, as well as their original rights to the lands they traditionally occupy."
48 "Most existing analysis assumes, explicitly or otherwise, that indigenous struggles and neoliberal ideologies stand fundamentally opposed to one another, that any convergences we might observe result either from unintended consequences of neoliberal reforms or from the prior achievements of indigenous resistance. [. . .] This assumption is incomplete and misleading, I contend, because it neglects a facet of the relationship that I will call 'neoliberal multiculturalism', whereby proponents of the neoliberal doctrine pro-actively endorse a substantive, if limited, version of indigenous cultural rights, as a means to resolve their own problems and advance their own political agendas." Charles Hale, "Does Multiculturalism Menace? Governance, Cultural Rights and the Politics of Identity in Guatemala," *Journal of Latin American Studies* (2002): 487.

Bibliography

Alviar Garcia, Helena. *Desarrollo, Teoría Feminista y Derecho: Propuestas para un análisis distributivo.* Bogotá: Ediciones Uniandes-Editorial Temis, 2008.
Alviar Garcia, Helena. *Italian Coffee: Retelling the Story.* (forthcoming publication 2021), 2020.

Alviar Garcia, Helena. "Leon Duguit's Influence in Colombia: The Last Opportunity of a Potentially Progressive Reform." In *Order From Transfer: Comparative Constitutional Design and Legal Culture*, edited by Günter Frankenberg, 306–21. Cheltenham: Edgar Elgar, 2013.

Alviar Garcia, Helena. "Looking beyond the Constitution: The Social and Biological Function of Property." In *Comparative Constitutional Law in Latin America*, edited by Rosalind Dixon and Tom Ginsburg. Cheltenham: Edgar Elgar, 2017.

Alviar Garcia, Helena. "The Classroom and the Clinic: The Relationship between Clinical Legal Education, Economic Development and Social Transformation." *UCLA Journal of International Law and Foreign Affairs* 13 (2008): 197–218.

Alviar Garcia, Helena. "The Unending Quest for Land: The Tale of Broken Constitutional Promises." *Texas Law Review* (2011): 1895–914.

Ankersen, T. Thomas, and Thomas Ruppert. "Tierra y Libertad: The Social Function Doctrine and Land Reform in Latin America." *Tulane Environmental Law Journal* (2006): 12–76.

BBC. "Can Free Market Economics Boost Amazonian Land Rights?" April 28, 2010. Accessed October 14, 2020. http://news.bbc.co.uk/2/hi/americas/8648699.stm.

Castro, Fidel. "Discurso ante el Pueblo Congregado en el Palacio Presidencial para Reafirmar su Apoyo al Gobierno Revolucionario y Como Protesta Contra la Cobarde Agresión Perpetrada Contra el Pacífico Pueblo de La Habana por Aviones Procedentes de Territorio Extranjero." La Habana, 1959. www.fidelcastro.cu/en/node/2624.

De Soto, Hernando. *The Other Path: The Economic Answer to Terrorism*. New York: Basic Books, 1989.

Dorner, Peter, and Herman Felstehausen. "Agrarian Reform and Employment: The Columbian Case." *International Labour Review* (1970): 221–40.

Esquirol, Jorge L. *Titling and Untitled Housing in Panama City*. Tennessee: Tennessee Journal of Law and Policy, 2014.

Findley, Roger W. *Ten Years of Land Reform in Colombia*. Madison, WI: Wisconsin Law Review, 1972.

Findley, Roger W. "Ten Years of Land Reform in Colombia." *Wisconsin Law Review* (1972): 880–923.

Hale, Charles. "Does Multiculturalism Menace? Governance, Cultural Rights and the Politics of Identity in Guatemala." *Journal of Latin American Studies* (2002): 487.

Hendrix, Steven E. "Tensions in Cuban Property Law." *Hastings International and Comparative Law Review* (1996): 16–39.

Hooker, Juliet. "Indigenous Inclusion/Black Exclusion: Race, Ethnicity and Multicultural Citizenship in Latin America." *Journal of Latin American Studies* (2005): 285.

Kenneth, Karst L. "The Colombian Land Reform Law: 'The Contribution of an Independent Judiciary.'" *The American Journal of Comparative Law* (1965): 118–24.

Mitchell, Timothy. "How Neoliberalism Makes its World: The Urban Property Rights Project in Peru." In *The Road from Mont Pèlerin: The Making of the Neoliberal Thought Collective*, edited by Philip Mirowski and Dieter Plehwe, 404. Boston: Harvard University Press, 2015.

Molina, Gerardo. *Las Ideas Liberales en Colombia: 1914–1934*. Bogotá: Tercer Mundo, 1984.

Monterroso, Iliana, Peter Cronkleton, Danny Pinedo, and Anne M. Larson. *Reclaiming Collective Rights: Land and Forest Tenure Reforms in Peru (1960–2016)*. Center for International Forestry Research, 2017.

Palacios, Marco. *Coffe in Colombia, 1850–1970*. Cambridge: Cambridge University Press, 1980.

Peñalver, Eduardo Moisés. "Redistributing Property: Natural law, International Norms and the Property Reforms of the Cuban Revolution." *Florida Law Review* (2000): 7.

Potter, Lesley. *Managing Oil Palm Landscapes: A Seven-country Survey of the Modern Palm Oil Industry in Southeast Asia, Latin America and West Africa*, 47–65. Report, Center for International Forestry Research, CIFOR, 2015.

Rulfo, Juan. *Pedro Páramo*. Translated by Lyzander Kemp. New York: Grove Weidenfield, 1990.

Stanfield, J. David, and Steve E. Hendrix. "Ownership Insecurity in Nicaragua." *Capital University Law Review* (1993): 3–39.

Teubal, Miguel, and Mariana Ortega Breña. "Agrarian Reform and Social Movements in the Age of Globalization: Latin America at the Dawn of the Twenty-First Century, Latin American Perspectives." In *Peasant movements in latin america: Looking back, moving ahead*, edited by Cliff Welch and Bernardo Mançano Fernandes, 12. Thousand Oaks: Sage Journals, 2009.

Thiemann, Louis, and Max Spoor. "Beyond the 'Special Period': Land Reform, Supermarkets and the Prospects for Peasant-Driven Food Sovereignty in Post-Socialist Cuba (2008–2017)." *Canadian Journal of Development Studies* (2019): 548–50.

Thome, Joseph R. "Limiraciones de la Legislación Colombiana para Expropiar o Comprar Fincas con Destino de Parcelación." *Interamerican Law Review* (1996): 281–91.

Van Cott, Donna Lee. "Constitutional Reform and Ethnic Rights in Latin America." *Parliamentary Affair* (2000): 45.

Yohannes, Okbazghi. "The Biofuel Industrial Complex and Its Migration to the Global South." In *The Biofuels Deception: Going Hungry on the Green Carbon Diet*, 71–132. New York: New York University Press, 2018.

3 Women and economic development

Determined by reproductive work

Many women in Latin America have been marginalized and at times excluded by the different models of economic development described in the two previous chapters. As a consequence, a question asked by legislators, activists and academics across the region is how to pinpoint the causes for this exclusion and design adequate solutions. This chapter analyzes different theoretical interpretations and their corresponding proposals.

The Lost Child by Elena Ferrante provides an apt starting point for the ideological debate regarding the unequal distribution of power and resources in Latin America. In fact, Elena Ferrante's novels foreground the difficulties, ambivalent feelings of motherhood and the work it entails. She brilliantly lays out what many women will identify with: the pull of attachment along with a strong desire to disentangle; the goal to protect and care for our children and partners laced with streaks of selfishness. This circumstance is not unique to the women from Naples Ferrante describes in her books but could arguably extended to the experience of motherhood in many contemporary societies in the region. Take for example the Leda, the narrator in *The Lost Daughter* who vividly describes this harrowing sensation: "All the hopes of youth seemed to have been destroyed, I seemed to be falling backward toward my mother, my grandmother, the chain of mute or angry women I came from."[1] Later on, Leda explains how giving birth and taking care of children is such a relentless task that women find themselves imagining other possible worlds as they reject their offspring:

> I felt their gazes longing to tame me, but more brilliant was the brightness of the life outside them, new colors, new bodies, new intelligence, a language to possess finally as if it were my true language, and nothing, nothing that seemed to me reconcilable with that domestic space from which they stared at me in expectation. Ah, to make them invisible, to no longer hear the demands of their flesh as commands more pressing, more powerful than those which came from mine.

[. . .] [2]
I loved them too much and it seemed to me that love for them would
keep me from becoming myself.

(Ferrante 2016)[3]

Ferrante's work is ultimately about how women are shaped, distorted and
many times destroyed by the social demands upon their bodies, mostly
through motherhood but more broadly through care work. These insights
are extremely relevant when we think about women's access to resources
and work. In Latin America, this has been delineated by the discussion
surrounding how to include them in the benefits of economic development. As it is advanced in the following pages, at the center of all of the
approaches, motherhood and care many times determine policy design and
outcome.

In addition to centering the importance of reproductive work in the
economic development agenda, the chapter analyzes the limits of the liberal feminist program; the challenges faced by the adoption of the term
gender and the difficulties encountered by indigenous feminists when
carving out a set of legal and regulatory moves that are tailored particularly for them.

In order to unveil the relationship between work and care, this chapter has
three parts. The first one discusses the theoretical debates regarding feminist
contributions to development: liberal, Marxist and the critique of the binary
character of feminism in the form of the gender and development along with
its contribution to indigenous feminism. Then, the cases of Colombia, Cuba
and Bolivia are discussed as model types of each one of these perspectives.
As it is the case in all the chapters of this book, the countries are used as
archetypes or models and are not intended to be comprehensive descriptions
of their legislations. The chapter ends with some thoughts on the role of
reproductive work and the insights of Ferrante.

Feminist contributions to development

Liberal feminism

The discussion surrounding the relationship between women and economic
development dates back to the early 1970s, after Esther Boserup's ground-
breaking work: "Woman's Role in Economic Development" (Boserup
1970).[4] In it, Boserup explored the gendered division of labor in relation to
agricultural production and the importance of women in subsistence production. These two facts became essential in understanding women's relevance in any development model.

Boserup's work is framed within the intellectual tradition dedicated to exploring the paths to reach economic development that had as its starting point accepting the benefits of a capitalist style of production. According to this view, once the process of modernization and industrialization are set off (with adequate state intervention) what followed was a straightforward, incremental process. The work of W.W. Rostow is one example of this view. He argued that economic development entailed a movement from the traditional to the modern through five identifiable stages: "the traditional society, the preconditions for take-off, the take-off, the drive to maturity, and the age of high mass-consumption" (Rostow 2015). Later in his explanation of this theory, Rostow argues that an increased capital accumulation would trigger a modernization process that in turn transformed social values, the way that politics was exercised, practiced and thought of, along with major shifts in institutional arrangements and cultural practices.

For some time, scant research was advanced regarding the differential effects that modernization had upon women. It was assumed that this process would benefit them equally. Industrialization and urbanization would increase work opportunities for them. Cultural change would follow the more modern a society was. This meant growing acceptance of equality between men and women, which in turn would be translated into more diverse job opportunities and an increase in freedoms, including access to birth control coupled with a capacity to decide over lifestyle and when or if to marry. When evidence showed that these patterns were not changing in the face of industrialization and growth, the preferred explanation was a backward culture: the persistence of male-centered traditional societies.

Boserup was inspired by a tradition of liberal feminists interested in unveiling women's status in different settings. Along with this goal, liberal feminists at the time were deeply interested in understanding how greater societal transformations (such as modernization and industrialization) had differentiated impact on women. A product of their research was a critique of the neutrality of economic development policies. Liberal feminists, among them Boserup, honed into the benefits of modernization, industrialization and urbanization. What they found (instead of the promised benefits for women) was a range of challenges: being excluded from jobs in subsistence farming and forced to enter a labor market where they were underpaid and discriminated. The existence of stereotypes about which jobs they could or could not do along with lower levels of education forced women to be employed in the lowest paid and most precarious jobs. This in turn increased their dependency on the male breadwinner within the household. Finally, liberal feminists analyzing women's role in economic development showed how most policies were designed to benefit this male breadwinner.[5] The few existing policies designed exclusively for women were geared to support their role as care givers (through nutritional and maternal child health programs), potential mothers (through population control projects) and small agricultural producers of food for household consumption. Boserup provided the empirical evidence to show how women were being effectively marginalized by development policies and programs. She compared farming systems and gender roles in Africa, Asia and Latin America, demonstrating that women developed, led and were in charge of different tasks, thus there was nothing natural or inevitable about the division of labor in agriculture, which described women as care givers and men as food producers. Along the way, she shed light upon women's heavy burden of care work and their invisibility in national statistics.

A product of her research and particular interpretation, the liberal feminist solution was to propose legal and administrative transformations guaranteeing women access to what was understood to be productive work and its financial benefits. These legal transformations encompassed equal rights amendments in constitutions, quotas in agricultural policies and plans, the inclusion of reproductive work in national accounts and the study of female heads of households. Ultimately, the objective was women's equal participation in the prevailing capitalist system, with little or no attempt to redefine economic development simply as growth. As a consequence, the research of liberal feminists is centered upon discrimination and how discrimination is economically irrational. If women are excluded from the benefits of economic development, half of the population will be unable to buy, exchange and in turn trigger growth. These themes are revisited later in the analysis of the case of Colombia as an example of the liberal feminist agenda in economic development.

Feminism influenced by Marxism and Dependency Theory

For feminists influenced by Marxism, what really affects women is the sexual division of labor, typical of capitalist production, which has expropriated their unpaid work. Their research is inspired by the work of Frederich Engels in *The Origins of the Family: Private Property and the State,*[6] where he argues that initial capitalist accumulation was male dominated. The text describes how the surplus of wealth created in agriculture and exchange was dominated by men. The accumulation of this surplus, in turn, was the foundation for private property. Women were highly absent from these two processes, as they were mostly in charge of the survival of the household through cooking, cleaning and generally taking care of others. In other words, producing goods not for exchange but for subsistence. As a result, women had little access to resources outside the household and this increased their dependency on men. According to this Marxist view, it is this unpaid care work (which guarantees the reproduction of the labor force) that makes it possible to pay workers very low salaries and paves the way for capital accumulation. The fact that women and children at times enter the labor market, creates a surplus of labor that in turn undermines the solidarity of the working class and lowers wages. In addition, Marxists are keen to highlight that capitalist accumulation is possible as a result of the separation of the worker from what he produces, which makes survival dependent on the, at times, erratic conditions of wage work.

Linking these insights to economic development, Boserup's work is criticized by Marxist feminists for accepting the promises of modernization, taking for granted the separation between productive and reproductive spheres and for defining economic development simply as growth. For liberal feminists, the problem with economic development programs and policies was discrimination, not that the model as such was initially flawed, as it promotes capitalist accumulation that adversely affects women. In terms of reproductive work, Marxist feminists argue that only when housework as well as the care of children and older adults is understood as national, public affairs will women be truly equal. For them, it does not matter how many anti-discrimination policies you pass, or how many equality clauses exist for the productive sphere, if you do not eliminate women's burden in the reproductive arena and the patriarchal system that allows it, no law or policy will make a difference. Their critique to the liberal formula is adequately summarized in the work of Lourdes Benería and Gita Sen:

> Radical policy would involve elimination of the hierarchical structure of production, perhaps by some form of workers' control and equalization of wages. To the extent that this would eliminate or reduce differences by sex. A less radical policy would involve equal opportunity/ affirmative action plans that take the structure of production and the labor hierarchy as a given but would make each job equally accessible to men and women. Both of these policies have a major flaw; they focus only on the structure of production and do not take into consideration women's role in the area of reproduction. If women face a double day and if child-care facilities are not available to them, neither of the two policies is likely to solve fully the problem of women's secondary status in the labor market, given that their participation in paid production is conditioned by their work in and around the household.
>
> (Benería and Sen 1982)

In addition to proposing the focus on the forms of capitalist accumulation, how it determines women's access to resources and the role of reproductive work in this equation, Marxist feminists have a deep interest in unveiling how class diversity has a differentiated impact. It is not the same to be a domestic worker in an urban setting; a waged rural laborer; a seasonal agricultural worker; an accountant, schoolteacher or nurse. As Benería and Sen aptly put it:

> Two implications concerning differences among women follow from our discussion thus far. First, a woman's class position structures the concrete meaning of her gender. The variations that exist between women's different classes are at least as important for the women's social position as the commonalities inherent in being a woman within a given society. Second, class defines the relations among women themselves. That is, class is not simply a differentiating mechanism that places women in varying social boxes. It is an antagonistic social relation that defines, for example, the oppressive relations between female domestic servants and their mistresses (Benería and Sen 1982).

(de Beauvoir 1973)

An additional and final layer to this perspective is a critique of colonialism and its effects on gender relations. The consequences of economic development as growth and capital accumulation were very specific for women in the Global South (including Latin America). As poor women lose control over land, water, fuel and food because of changes in models of production (from subsistence to producing for the market or for export), women also see an increase in their workload as they have to look farther for water, fuel and, in some cases, food. In addition, when agrobusiness takes over an area, women could be forced to be seasonal workers, affecting other sources of possible income, or not be employed at all.

Gender and development

The critique of the binary, sex-centered approach of some feminists involved in the development field led to the incorporation of the term "gender." Its starting point is the insight that taking women as a category is too essentialist, frozen in time, and as a consequence, loses sight of the dynamic character and relational form in which men and women interact with each other as well as with society. It is inspired by the work of anthropologists who had been researching the range of gender identities that formed around males and females across cultural borders. This in turn meant that there was nothing natural or determinant in biological differences, but that gender was socially constructed as in Simone de Beauvoir's famous phrase, "one is not born a woman, but rather becomes one" (de Beauvoir 1973).

Thinking in terms of gender meant that economic development programs designed to provide aid to women should move beyond providing assistance in themes that were considered specifically their domain, such as family planning, household management, cooking, child rearing and education. Gender includes the idea of a continuum. In other words, no individual is purely feminine or masculine. As a consequence, attention should be paid to men who are excluded because they embrace women's traits, jobs or attitudes, and it should be accepted that patriarchy is a cage for both men and women. Unveiling the relations between men and women also allowed a broadening of the scope of economic development, from productive initiatives to the incorporation of issues such as environmental degradation and conservation. A critique of modernization and the effects of colonialism were central to this analysis as well,[7] as the rigidities of the dichotomy separating the sexes was an imposition on Latin American indigenous cultures that were based on complementarity and not difference, as will be explained later.

Finally, there are a few risks that evolve from the incorporation of the term "gender." First, it brought with it a tension within feminism, as it tried to strike a balance between difference while it looks for what are the common themes that unite a struggle. On the other hand, the term could just replace the word "women" with little commitment to incorporate ideas about the cultural and historical nature of its analysis along with its transformative potential.

Indigenous feminism

Indigenous women's movements have been strong in Latin America at least since the early 1990s. At the center of their struggle are fairer relations between men and women and a critique of the rational, autonomous individual, distinct from the natural environment so central to Western, liberal thought. This centrality of the individual is replaced by an emphasis on the complementarity between genders as well as a less anthropocentric view of nature. Despite the fact that indigenous women's movements are united with broader indigenous movements in denouncing the cruelty and legacy of colonialism as well as current forms of exclusion and exploitation, they are also demanding that their own communities and organizations change attitudes and practices that continue to exclude and oppress women.

Indigenous women are at the intersection of typical feminist claims along with the demands of the indigenous people they belong to. This creates a tension regarding where their alliance must stand with men within indigenous groups in terms of self-determination, the rights to a territory and the right to participate politically at the national level. The feminist agenda also includes calls for greater equality, ending violence against women and providing them with access to resources within their own communities. Different indigenous feminist groups will have distinct ways to achieve better resource distribution across gender lines. I would argue there is a continuum between, on the one side, groups whose claims are framed within liberal feminism and at the other extreme groups that center their demands not upon equality but upon a strengthening of the complementarity among sexes. A liberal feminist example would be the Zapatista's Women Revolutionary Law, which includes the rights to political participation and to occupy leading roles within their political institutions, a life free of sexual and domestic violence, the capacity to decide when and how many children to have, to a fair wage, to choose a partner, to have an education and to the right to health.[8] At the other extreme of the spectrum one can find movements that have pushed against liberal definitions of gender equality and tried to promote the coexistence of gender in public and private spheres.[9]

The interaction with liberal feminists has triggered a debate within the indigenous women's movement about how much influence urban, white feminists should have in the terms of their struggle. Some within the indigenous movement consider liberal feminism essentialist, as it understands only one dimension of women, it is conservative because it is culturally imperialist and it centers emancipation only upon the existence of rights, not proposing sweeping structural transformations and buying into liberal ideas of emancipation.[10]

In addition to this tension between an indigenous view of the world and Western ideas of women's emancipation in the form of rights, there have been diverse interpretations of the term *Buen Vivir*, Good Living, central to the idea of complementarity. *Buen vivir* has been defended as an important indigenous contribution to debates about economic development.

Some have stated that this indigenous concept is a Latin American contribution as important as the insights provided by *dependentista* analysis. The term has been generally defined as "living in harmony with oneself (identity), with society (equity) and with nature (sustainability)" (Hidalgo Capitan and Cubillo-Guevara 2017, 25). Academics Hidalgo Capital and Cubillo Guevara argue that far from being a monolithic concept, there three are different ideological strands: "an indigenist and *pachamamist* (which prioritizes identity as an objective), one which is socialist and statist (which prioritizes equity) and another which is 'ecologist' and 'post-developmentalist' (which prioritizes sustainability)" (Hidalgo Capitan and Cubillo-Guevara 2017, 27). The indigenist perspective concentrates on a critique of modernization and economic development as a universal goal. Their quite conservative view of the world promotes reproducing the living conditions that prevailed in pre-colonial times for the peoples of the continent. The main ideal is to protect and strengthen the self-determination of indigenous peoples by including in the acceptance of pluricultural states in constitutions, recuperating ancestral traditions and foregrounding the spiritual dimensions of *Buen Vivir* (Hidalgo Capitan and Cubillo-Guevara 2017). The socialist, state-centered view proposes a new economic development model that improves the distribution of resources initially supported by extractivism. The state is in charge of defining *Buen Vivir*, which includes being a post-capitalist society characterized by solidarity, an "economy with a market and not a market economy" (Hidalgo Capitan and Cubillo-Guevara 2017). Finally, there is the ecologist perspective, which is less state centered and where local communities can define what they understand to be a Good Living and include a system that is centered around nature (Hidalgo Capitan and Cubillo-Guevara 2017).

Contemporary feminist debates on economic development: diverse critiques of neoliberalism

Liberal feminists have criticized neoliberalism for not being liberal enough in relationship to women. For this group of academics, neoliberalism does not do enough to promote equality or to eliminate the conditions that make inequality possible. Their critique concentrates on stating the reasons why women cannot enter the market in equal conditions as their male counterparts. Neoliberalism has been able to incorporate most of these critiques within its normative content. A result of this, employment and political discrimination have been banned, quota laws have been included and legislation against domestic violence (Alviar Garcia, Violence Against Women as an Economic Issue: making sense of a fragmented field 2016) has been discussed in both international forums as well as in local legal and regulatory agendas.

Marxist feminists have concentrated their efforts on describing the negative effects of state reduction and privatization. Among the elements of this analysis is the observation that the state has historically employed more women than the private sector. Most of this research was done in former socialist countries in Eastern Europe, where work generated by the state was a way of giving real opportunities and equal treatment to women. This was done by including them in diverse jobs beyond those they traditionally occupied, such as nursing and education, and forcefully including them in technical, industrial and agricultural tasks (Meurs 1997).[11] As the state reduced its size and was replaced by the market, women suffered higher rates of unemployment. Not only did women lose their jobs, but there was a male backlash to retrieve their dominating role as main providers (Goven 1992).

On the other hand, Marxist feminists have also analyzed the types and quality of jobs generated by the export led growth model. Flexibility, long hours, meager wages and the lack of job security are some of the main characteristics of the type of jobs generated when economic development programs shifted to the promotion of free trade and export-led growth. According to a range of studies, these jobs are mostly female because women are considered more docile workers,[12] are not members of unions and have "natural" talents for these types of industries such as flower exports and maquiladoras (Folbre, Bergmann, and Floro 1992). Other research has focused on criticizing the dismantling of social policies, showing how women are hit harder by this. The main argument is that when neoliberalism eliminates social assistance provided by the state, poverty increases, and because women are on average poorer than men (Deere, Safa, and Antrobus 1997) (McCluskey 2003), neoliberalism ends up affecting them more.

Gender and development feminists continue to call for a more dynamic relational approach, unveiling of the negative effects of neoliberalism and could also be applied (as I will describe further along) to the disappointment of the Cuban socialist experiment. Indigenous women's movements have been able to translate their ideas into constitutional reforms in countries such as Ecuador and Bolivia but have not seen the sweeping advancement they were expecting.

The following section briefly takes some archetypes to illustrate three issues that have been on the agenda of feminists: women's participation in rural development programs as an example of the feminist, liberal agenda; access to state-funded care illustrating the feminist, Marxist approach and the participation and transformations that indigenous women gained in the drafting of the 2009 Bolivian Constitution. The cases are not intended to draw a full, comprehensive picture. In each one of the countries there are important efforts of academics and policy makers to promote different agendas to the right or the left that are not discussed in the chapter, as Colombia, Cuba and Bolivia are used as examples. Therefore, the intention is to describe the countries as examples of political theories that underlie the inclusion of women in economic development goals and at the same time sketch some challenges each one of these ideological models face.

Including women in rural development: an example of liberal feminism

In Colombia, there are a number of laws and regulations aimed at protecting – and, in many cases, privileging – women's access to resources and economic development policies. Nevertheless, women continue to have less access to rural property, earn less in rural areas, and are overrepresented among the extremely poor.[13] Colombia is an example of a liberal feminist approach centered upon equality in the productive sphere and defining discrimination as the main harm, with little concern for the burden of reproductive work. At the same time, conservatives have managed to attack the incorporation of the term "gender" to economic development policies. In fact, conservative groups have been gaining ground by stating that the left has a gender ideology agenda aimed at ending the family relations, the institution of marriage, the right to life and religious freedom.[14]

The Colombian Constitution has a number of articles aimed at reaching equality between men and women. The first is the equality clause contained in Article 13.[15] This article has two separate sections. The first establishes the prohibition of discrimination, thereby codifying a negative definition of equality.[16] The second section in Article 13 provides a positive view of equality, one that requires the state to act.[17] This section has been the basis for laws aimed at correcting unequal representation and participation of women.[18] Along with the general equality clause, Article 43 of the constitution expressly reaffirms equality between men and women.[19] In terms of access to rural development, there are a few other provisions to take into account. Articles 64,[20] 65,[21] and 80[22] establish special state protection for rural workers and food production and determine that the state should do its best to guarantee sustainable development in order to protect its resources.[23]

Along with constitutional provisions, there are a number of laws that reiterate equality. These include quotas,[24] the criminalization of violence against women,[25] the reiteration of equal salaries,[26] the accounting of reproductive work[27] and the special protection of women heads of households.[28] Specifically in relation to women and rural development, there have been a long list of laws, among them Law 160 of 1994, known in Colombia as the Agricultural Reform Law. The objective of the law (as has been a trend in all agrarian reform laws since the early twentieth century[29]) is to transform the existing land concentration.[30] In addition (and also as most agrarian laws since the early 1980s), it explicitly establishes that women will have equal access to the policies of agricultural development.[31] Another relevant law is Law 731 of 2002, which aims at improving rural women's quality of life.[32] It covers a variety of issues, most importantly women's access to land titling, credit and education.[33]

Multilateral organizations have been determinant in framing Colombian government initiatives related to improving women's conditions in rural areas. A recent report in which United Nations Food and Agriculture Organization (FAO) participates highlighted the importance of women in the productive structure of agriculture, notwithstanding the lack of equality between men and women in the rural areas.[34]

These policies have also been reflected in Colombia's recent legal developments regarding the peace process. For example, the land restitution law establishes gender inequality as one of its guiding principles when granting humanitarian aid measures, comprehensive care, assistance and reparation.[35] The aim is to end discrimination.

In addition, legislation regarding women's access to land and agrarian policy has a section that determines preferential access for women in the land restitution processes.[36] The "Comprehensive Rural Reform" established that women would be recognized as independent citizens with rights who had equal footing to men in relationship to access to property, access to public funding and training. In addition, the law stated that institutions that had contributed to block women from obtaining equal access would be dismantled.[37]

None of these policies have significantly shifted access to resources and power for rural women as much of the research demonstrates. In previous work I have argued that this lack of meaningful transformation is due to the interaction economic development plans that privilege agri-business which mostly employs men, family law (Alviar Garcia, Legal Reform, Social Policy, and Gendered Redistribution in Columbia: The Role of the Family 2011) and cultural norms regarding the role of women within the household and in society.[38]

The search for equality in Cuba

Since its initial stages, the Cuban revolution was described by its leaders as having the goal to end oppression for many in the country. In one of the many speeches in which he referred to this topic, Fidel Castro argued that the Revolution had helped move away from discrimination and that the struggle against capitalism would also end race and class inequality:

> I don't know if you remember in our previous bourgeoise constitution, there was an article that declared the illegality of any form of discrimination on the basis of race or sex . . . but a constitution or an article in a constitution within a capitalist society doesn't solve a thing, because there continued to be discrimination in both terms of sex and race. Above all that there was a classist society, a society based on exploitation.
>
> Race and Sex discrimination cannot end in a class centered society, in a society of some exploiters and some who are exploited. Discrimination based on race and sex has ended in our country because exploitation has finished.
>
> (Castro 1966)

Later on, in the same 1966 speech, he accepts that equality between men and women has not been reached, and as a well-educated Marxist, he explains the difficulties faced by women because of their reproductive work duties:

> Now, it is precisely because of this nature endowed function on women that place an extraordinary duty, that enslaves them with household chores. . . . Here for example we have a billboard that states: "A million women will be in the productive sector by 1970." Unfortunately, this goal for 1970 will be impossible to reach. Why? Because in order to have a million women in production we need thousands of child-care sites, thousands of elementary and boarding schools, thousands of worker's dining rooms, thousands of social services. [. . .]
>
> In other words, in order to liberate women from all care activities that enslave her, that prevent her from entering the labor force or engaging in other essential activities of society, we need to provide all of these.
>
> (Castro 1966)

Cuba established the constitutional structure and legal polices to promote women's equality. Articles 41 and 42 of the 1976 Constitution established equal rights for men and women and punished discrimination based on race, skin color, sex, national origin, religious beliefs or any other attack over human dignity.[39] In addition, the Criminal Code establishes that any violation of the right to equality is a crime that would be punishable with up to two years in jail.[40] The labor code specifically protects working mothers: "the employer shall establish and maintain working conditions for women that take into account their participation in the workforce and their social function as mothers."[41] During the first three months of maternity leave, they receive their full salary, after that they may extend the leave to nine unpaid months.[42] After that year they are automatically placed in their previous job.[43]

Women have a range of other rights, such as free and full access to abortion, contraception and prenatal care; the family code of 1975 establishes that there should be an equal division of tasks within the household;[44] day care centers are theoretically available for everyone; getting a divorce is relatively easy (Murphy et al. 1991). Women also receive equal access to education at all levels, and as early as the late 1970s women held two-thirds of technical and professional jobs.[45] In 2006, they represented 60% of all faculty members in universities, 50% of all scientists, 52% of physicians and 51% of lawyers (Nuñez Sarmiento 2010).

Despite all of these constitutional and legislative achievements, women continue to be burdened by reproductive work. Research advanced by the Cuban National Office of Statistics unequivocally showed that women carried the brunt of it. They reported that they dedicate 36 hours a week of housework, while men reported 12 hours:

> Cuban women are judges, professors, scientists, physicians and blue-collar workers, but they are also the ones who iron, cook and clean the homes. Men dedicate their time to shopping, paying the bills, and putting the garbage out.
>
> (Nuñez Sarmiento 2010)

Social scientists studying this difference argue that it is due to the fact that women do not assign care duties to male members of the family.[46] In addition, despite changes in attitudes and stereotypes about women as they joined the labor force, discussions about maleness and what it means to be a man have lagged behind. Scholar Martha Nuñez Sarmiento, who has studied the situation of working women on the island for more than 25 years, explains how within the household men continue to be very patriarchal and women are complicit in this because of the way they educate their sons.[47]

Along with demands of a society that is still very patriarchal, other scholars have explored the demands imposed upon women by the Cuban state and the consequences this has over gender relations. Elise Andaya's in-depth study of sexual and reproductive rights in the book *Post-Soviet Cuba, Conceiving Cuba: Reproduction, Women and the State in Post-Soviet Era* (Andaya 2014) explains how traditional socialist governments historically aim to link the state to women:

> In socialist theory, state support for reproduction and the de-gendering of the productive and reproductive spheres would form the basis for new and egalitarian norms of female and male socialist citizenship both home and in the workplace. In practice the lives of my informants showed, while women assumed many new roles and obligations outside the home, the connection between women and reproduction remained largely intact, women's supposedly natural affinity for nurturance and reproductive labor was often tacitly reaffirmed at both the level of the state and familial gender relations. Thus, socialism's new woman has been produced not simply through explicit policies around labor or childcare, but also indirectly through women's double and triple burdens as mothers, workers, and revolutionaries.
>
> (Andaya 2014)

Anaya interestingly describes how, despite the fact that Cuba continues to be a socialist country, during the Special Period, the amount of hours it took for a household to get the goods and services it required (that were no longer provided by the state) was mostly shouldered by women (Andaya 2014).

In addition, even in more prosperous times access to childcare was never total. In 1997, only 20% of working women had access to it (Andaya 2014). Grandmothers still do much of the childcare duties of working mothers. As it happens in many other places, women are also in charge of taking care of the elderly or those who are very ill. Given this continued link between women and reproductive work, it is not surprising that those who have government-provided housing or childcare have a highly dependent relationship to the state, which limits their possibilities of engaging in more lucrative lines of work in other sectors of the economy.[48] It should come as no surprise, then, that women have much less access to other economic arrangements such as being a small business owner (only one out of four state-registered businesses are owned by women). A survival strategy for women is therefore to continue working for the government and taking a second job (Andaya 2014). Finally, and in a trend that is also typical of developed capitalist countries, women who are well off as a consequence of their partners income in private business or remittances decide to stay home.

Indigenous feminism in Bolivia: between gender complementarity and rights

In the search for greater equality of indigenous people and within them of indigenous women, women fared better than indigenous groups in the Bolivian constitutional process. Evo Morales, the first self-identified indigenous president was elected in 2005. His party, MAS (Movimiento hacia el Socialismo), had as its banner to defend the claims of the Bolivian indigenous community. After he was sworn in, many of his state ministers had an indigenous background and he demanded that state officials had to speak one of the three indigenous languages (Htun and Ossa 2013). MAS also included strict parity rules that led many women to be included politically and paved the way for Congress to approve parity laws for the National Electoral Court, the State Electoral Courts, the Constitutional Court and, importantly, for the selection of the leaders for indigenous regions (Htun and Ossa 2013). In addition, the contribution of indigenous and feminist movements in the Constitutional Assembly was quite strong according to many accounts.[49]

The strength of indigenous feminists was translated into the incorporation of an extensive bill of rights for women. Despite the participation of diverse feminist groups, they coalesced around a liberal definition of equality. Stéphanie Rousseau states that only 10% of female constituents identified with the complementarity principle:

> In a publication presenting interviews with eighty-four of eighty-five female constituents who were asked the question "What does 'gender' mean to you?" 24 percent answered by reference to equality, equity

and/or non-discrimination, whereas 20 percent referred to their own experience as women, 18 percent talked about political participation and 10 percent referred to the indigenous principle of complementarity.

(Rousseau 2011)

The 2009 Bolivian Constitution includes a range of rights aimed at women, promises of equality developed with anti-discrimination, violence against women and special provisions promoting women's access to resources, much in line with the liberal feminist agenda indigenous idea of complementarity.[50]

Conclusions

This chapter has illustrated the fundamental role that the interaction between productive and reproductive work plays in economic development policies. As the Colombian case illustrated, in designing economic development policies for rural women solely in terms of equal access to land and the elimination of discrimination, the results are meager. As long as there is little or no acknowledgment of how the burden of care work interacts with the productive sphere, the feminist liberal goal of equality is elusive. On the other hand, the case of Cuba exemplifies how constitutionally enshrining that reproductive tasks should be shared equally is insufficient if education and access to public resources are not transformed. In both cases, the insights of Elena Ferrante's regarding the ambivalence, difficulties and limitations of care work provide essential insights when trying to understand the limitations of public policy aimed at including women in economic development models.

The chapter also sheds light upon the difficulties of translating into constitutional provisions ideas about gender and complementarity between sexes promoted by indigenous feminists. Along this same line, indigenous feminists confront challenges of attacking the patriarchal, authoritarian manifestations of indigenous men and at the same time acknowledging that they share equal levels of dispossession.

Notes

1   Elena Ferrante, *The Lost Daughter* (New York: Europa Editions, 2016), 57.
2   Ibid., 83.
3   Ibid., 96.
4   As Tinker points out: "In 1970 the General Assembly included in the International Development Strategy a phrase – later widely copied – which stated the importance of encouraging 'full integration of women in the total development effort.' In 1974 the SID/WID produced a bibliography, a mere five pages long,

and in the process 'discovered' Ester Boserup's Women's Role in Economic Development. Her book was instantly embraced because Boserup's theory legitimized efforts to influence policy development with a combined argument for justice and efficiency." Irene Tinker, "The Making of a Field: Advocates, Practitioners and Scholars," in *The Women Gender and Development Reader*, ed. T. Nalini Visvanathan, Lynn Dugan, Laurie Nisonoff, and Nan Wiegerma (London: Zed Books, 1997).

5 For more on this historical privileging of the male breadwinner, see Helena Alviar Garcia, *Engulfed by the Family: Women in the Colombian Development State between 1966 and 1990* Rev. direito GV [online]. 2015, vol. 11, n.2, pp. 365–390. ISSN 2317–6172.

6 "In the old communistic household, which embraced numerous couples and their children, the administration of the household, entrusted to the women, was just as much a public, socially necessary industry as the providing of food by men. This situation changed with the patriarchal family, and even more with the monogamian individual family. The administration of the household lost its public character. It was no longer the concern of society. It became a private service. The wife became the first domestic servant, pushed out of participation of social production." Friedrich Engels, "The Origin of the Family, Private Property and State," in *The Marx-Engels Reader*, ed. Robert C. Tucke (New York: Norton, 1978), 744.

7 Many authors have voiced this critique. My favorite is Edward Said: "My contention is that without examining Orientalism as a discourse one cannot possibly understand the enormously systematic discipline by which European culture was able to manage -and even produce- the Orient politically, sociologically, militarily, ideologically, scientifically and imaginatively during the post-Enlightenment period." Edward Said, "Orientalism," in *The Post-Colonial Studies Reader*, ed. Bill Ashcroft, Gareth Griffiths and Helen Tiffin (London: Routledge, 1997), 88–89.

8 Zapatista Women's Revolutionary Law: "First – Women, regardless of their race, creed, color or political affiliation, have the right to participate in the revolutionary struggle in any way that their desire and capacity determine. Second – Women have the right to work and receive a just salary. Third – Women have the right to decide the number of children they have and care for. Fourth – Women have the right to participate in the matters of the community and have charge if they are free and democratically elected. Fifth – Women and their children have the right to Primary Attention in their health and nutrition. Sixth – Women have the right to education. Seventh – Women have the right to choose their partner and are not obliged to enter into marriage. Eighth – Women have the right to be free of violence from both relatives and strangers. Rape and attempted rape will be severely punished. Ninth – Women will be able to occupy positions of leadership in the organization and hold military ranks in the revolutionary armed forces. Tenth – Women will have all the rights and obligations which the revolutionary laws and regulations give." Zapatista Army of National Liberation (Ejército Zapatista de Liberación Nacional), The Zapatista Women's Revolutionary Law, Chiapas, Mexico: January 1, 1994.

9 For more on the diverse interactions between feminists, indigenous and peasant women, see Stéphanie Rousseau, "Indigenous and Feminist Movements at the Constituent Assembly in Bolivia: Locating the Representation of Indigenous Women," *Latin American Research Review* (2011): 5–28.

10 One of the manifestations of this tension is with customary law, which at times is at odds with indigenous women's rights: "One of the most immediate tensions revolves around the revaluation of customary law that is part of the project of indigenous cultural recognition and political autonomy. Customary practices do not always embody indigenous women's rights or aspirations, thus their interest in participating in the (re)definition of what are to be considered indigenous norms." Stéphanie Rousseau, p. 9.

11 Another article that deals with this topic is Toni Makkai, "Social Policy and Gender in Eastern Europe," in *Gendering Welfare State*, ed. Diane Sainsbury (Thousand Oaks: Sage Publications, 1994), 188–206.

12 For more on the economic determinants of women's docility, see Diane Elson and Ruth Pearson, "The Subordination of Women and the Internationalization of Factory Production," in *The Women, Gender and Development Reader*, ed. Nalini Visvanathan, Lynn Duggan, Laurie Nisonnof and Jan Wiegersma (London: Zen Books, 1997), 191–203.

13 *See* Ministry of Agriculture, "Situación de las mujeres rurales en Colombia (2010–2018)" (2018), www.minagricultura.gov.co/ministerio/direcciones/Documents/Situacion%20de%20las%20mujeres%20rurales%20en%20Colombia%20 2010-2018.pdf ("40.4% of rural households with female heads are poor due to deprivation in their living conditions (multidimensional poverty), compared to 33.6% of rural households with male heads and 12.4% of urban households with female leadership. 40.5% of people in rural households with female heads are in monetary poverty, compared to 34.7% of people in rural households with male heads and 27.6% in urban households with female heads. 19.8% of people in rural households with female heads are in extreme monetary poverty, compared to 14.0% of people in rural households with male heads and 6.6% in urban households with female heads. Only 40.7% of rural women participate in the labor market compared to 76.1% of rural men and 57.2% of urban women. Rural women face a higher unemployment rate (8.9%) compared to men (3.0%).").

14 One of the leading right-wing figures in the country, Alejandro Ordoñez argued that the Colombian Peace process should be defeated in a referendum, because it advanced gender ideology: "From Havana they have been designing public policy based on gender ideology to redesign family, marriage, the right to life and freedom of religion in our legislation." Revista Semana, "El polémico video de Alejandro Ordóñez sobre la ideología de género y la paz," *Revista Semana*, September 2016.

15 "All persons are born free and equal before the law, shall receive equal protection and treatment from the authorities, and shall enjoy the same rights, freedoms, and opportunities without any discrimination on account of gender, race, national or family origin, language, religion, [and] political or philosophical opinion." POLITICAL COLOMBIAN CONSTITUTION OF 1991 [C.P.] Article 13, *translated in* Anna I. Vellve Torras, Jefri J. Ruchti and Maria del Carmen Gress, trans., POLITICAL CONSTITUTION OF COLOMBIA OF 1991, as consolidated to Legislative Act No. 6 (November 24, 2011) (HeinOnline World Constitutions Illustrated library 2011), http://unpan1.un.org/intradoc/groups/public/documents/un-dpadm/unpan048941~1.pdf.

16 In ruling C-371 of 2000, the Court reviewed some of its decisions based on the first section of the article and defined its negative aspect:

[This Court] has found that establishing a marriage annulment clause only applied to women; completely denying access to women to the only military academy existing in the country; allowing only men to affiliate their spouses to the social security system; establishing that the only residence for marriage is where the woman lives and forbidding women from working night shifts, all go against the equality clause. In all of these events, the Court concluded that differences in the law . . . perpetuate cultural prejudices and promote a harmful idea . . . that women are inferior to men.

Corte Constitucional [C.C.] [Constitutional Court], marzo 19, 2000, Sentencia C-371/00, Gaceta de la Corte Constitutcional [G.C.C.]

17 "The State shall promote the conditions so that equality may be real and effective and shall adopt measures in favor of the discriminated or [of] marginalized groups," POLITICAL COLOMBIAN CONSTITUTION OF 1991 C.P.] Article 13.

18 The quota law for government posts is one example of these positive actions. *See* L. 581, May 31, 2000, [No. 44.026] DIARIO OFFICIAL [D.O.].

19 POLITICAL COLOMBIAN CONSTITUTION OF 1991 [C.P.] Article 43 ("Women and men have equal rights and opportunities. Women may not be subjected to any class of discrimination. During pregnancy and after delivery, women shall enjoy the special assistance and protection of the State and shall receive from it food subsidies if they are unemployed or without support [*desamparada*]. The State shall support in a special way the female head of household.").

20 POLITICAL COLOMBIAN CONSTITUTION OF 1991 [C.P.] Article 64 ("It is the duty of the State to promote the progressive access of agricultural workers to the ownership of land, in individual or associative form, and to the services of education, health, housing, social security, recreation, credit, communications, the commercialization of products, technical and managerial assistance, with the purpose of improving the incomes and quality of life of the peasants [*campesinos*].").

21 POLITICAL COLOMBIAN CONSTITUTION OF 1991 [C.P.] Article 65 ("The production of food shall enjoy the special protection of the State. For that purpose, priority shall be given to the integral development of agricultural, cattle, fishing, forestry, and agroindustrial activities, as well as to the building of works of physical infrastructure and to the suitability *[adecuatión]* of lands.").

22 POLITICAL COLOMBIAN CONSTITUTION OF 1991 [C.P.] Article 80 ("The State shall plan the handling and use of the natural resources in order to guarantee their sustainable development, their conservation, restoration, or substitution.").

23 *See* Final Agreement to End the Armed Conflict and Build a Stable and Lasting Peace (2016), p. 14: The final peace agreement, in the point referring to the "Comprehensive Rural Reform," establishes sustainable development as one of its guiding principles, "that is to say, development that is environmentally and socially sustainable, requiring protection and promotion of access to water, as part of an ordered concept of territory." Available in English at http://especiales.presidencia.gov.co/Documents/20170620-dejacion-armas/acuerdos/acuerdo-final-ingles.pdf.

24 L. 581, May 31, 2000 [No. 44.026] DIARIO OFICIAL [D.O].

25 L. 1257, December 4, 2008 [No. 47.193] DIARIO OFICIAL [D.O.].

26 L. 1496, December 29, 2011 [No. 48.297] DIARIO OFICIAL [D.O.].

27 L. 1413, November 11, 2010 [No. 47.890] DIARIO OFICIAL [D.O.].

28 L. 82, November 3, 1993 [No. 41.101] DIARIO OFICIAL [D.O.].

29 *See generally* Helena Alviar García, "The Unending Quest for Land: The Tale of Broken Constitutional Promises," *Texas Law Review* 1895, 89 (2011).

30 The first article of the law establishes that "reform the agricultural social structure through process oriented at preventing and eliminating the unequal

concentration of rural land or its anti-economic fracturing," and to "support men and women peasants with low income in their process of acquiring lands by themselves through credit and direct subsidy." L. 160, August 3, 1994 [No. 41.479] DIARIO OFICIAL [D.O.].

31 The law specifically establishes this objective by stating that "the female peasant and indigenous population is guaranteed the same conditions and opportunities to participate equitably in the plans, programs and projects of agricultural development." Author's translation. *Id.*

32 Law 731 of 2002 states its objectives to "improve the quality of life of women in rural areas, specially low income women, and look[] for measures oriented at increasing equality among rural men and women." L. 731, January 14, 2002 [No. 44.678] DIARIO OFICIAL [D.O.].

33 As additional proof that the law in the books does not necessarily translate into transformations, this law includes three articles that are very similar to the ones found on today's restitution law:

"**Article 24. Titling of rural reform land to spouse or permanent companion in state of abandonment.** In cases where the land is titled or in the process of being so, to both spouse or permanent companions, or only to one of the spouses or permanent companions, in the event that one of them abandons the other, the rights over the land in the process of titling or already titled, will remain in the head of the spouse or permanent companion that proves the abandonment situation and that fulfills the requisites to demand prescription.

Article 25. Titling of land to communitarian associations or associative groups of women. Both Communitarian associations and associative groups of women that fulfill the requisites demanded by the law could be beneficiaries of the land titling process. In the same sense the preferential right over land is guaranteed to women head of the household and to those who are in a state of social and economic vulnerability due to violence, abandonment or widowhood.

Article 26. Equal participation of rural women in the process of adjudication and use of rural reform land. In all the processes of adjudication and use of the rural reform land that allow for the participation in decisions, training, and technical assistance and land price bargaining, women and men beneficiaries should intervene, with the object, of guaranteeing transparency and equality in those procedures."

L. 731, January 14, 2002 [No. 44.678] DIARIO OFICIAL [D.O.] (emphasis added).

34 Ministry of Agriculture, "Situación de las mujeres rurales en Colombia (2010–2018)" (2018), www.minagricultura.gov.co/ministerio/direcciones/Documents/Situacion%20de%20las%20mujeres%20rurales%20en%20Colombia%202010-2018.pdf.

35 L. 1448, June 10, 2011 No. 48.096, DIARIO OFICIAL [D.O.]. Article 13.

36 L. 1448, June 10, 2011 No. 48.096, DIARIO OFICIAL [D.O.]. Articles 114–118.

37 Final Agreement to End the Armed Conflict and Build a Stable and Lasting Peace (2016), p. 14. Available in English at http://especiales.presidencia.gov.co/Documents/20170620-dejacion-armas/acuerdos/acuerdo-final-ingles.pdf.

38 *See* Alviar Garcia, Helena "Legal Reform, Social Policy and Gendered Redistribution in Colombia: The Role of the Family" American University Journal of Gender Social Policy (2011), p. 593. ("Background rules allow one to understand how the definition of property, the enforcement of labor contracts, the criminal code, and family law all determine the outcomes of social policy. These rules frame the outcome because they effectively determine the bargaining power both between social

classes as well as among men and women."). *See also id.* at 599 ("[P]rogressives have underestimated the relevance of a powerful executive in the distribution of welfare benefits, the role that administrative agencies effectively have when defining rights, and the effect that labor, criminal and family judges have. This explains why redistributive social policies and gender equality norms are reiterated in the texts, but because their regulation comes late, it is insufficient or effectively blocks any weak re-distributional impulse the legal or constitutional text might have. In addition, many legislators have lost sight of the fact that norms are interrelated: labor law is related to property and criminal law; social policies are related to divorce laws, access to abortion, and the gendered labor market.").

39 Cuban Constitution (1976), Article 41 "All citizens enjoy equal rights and are subject to equal duties" and Article 42 "Discrimination on the basis of race, skin color, sex, national origin, religious beliefs and any other detrimental to human dignity is prohibited and punishable by law. State institutions educate everyone, from the earliest age, on the principle of equality of human beings."

40 Cuban Criminal Code, Article 295.1: "Anyone who discriminates against another person or promotes or incites discrimination (. . .) incurs a punishment of deprivation of freedom for six months to two years or a fine of two hundred to five hundred quotas or both."

41 Cuban Labor Code, Article 212: "Working women are guaranteed working conditions that are in harmony with their physical and physiological particularities, considering their decisive participation in work and recognizing their high social function as a mother."

42 Ibid., Article 218: "The woman worker is also entitled, by reason of maternity, to the grant of paid leave up to six weeks before delivery and twelve weeks after the same."

43 Ibid., Article 2019: "The labor entity must grant unpaid leave to those workers who require it, for the care of their minor children, provided that the requirements established by law are met (. . .), the worker is guaranteed the right to remain in the position she holds."

44 Cuban Family Code, Article 26: "Both spouses are obliged to care for the family they have created and to cooperate with each other in the education, training and guidance of children in accordance with the principles of socialist morality. Likewise, to the extent of the capabilities or possibilities of each one, they must participate in the government of the home and cooperate in its best development." And Article 27: "The spouses are obliged to contribute to the satisfaction of the needs of the family that they have created with their marriage, each according to their faculties and economic capacity. However, if any of them only contributes to that subsistence with their work in the home and in the care of the children, the other spouse must contribute by himself to the said subsistence, without prejudice to the duty to cooperate to said work and care."

45 For more on these transformations, Helen Safa, "Female Headed Households and Poverty in Latin America: A Comparison of Cuba, Puerto Rico, and the Dominican Republic," in *Women's Activism in Latin America and the Caribbean*, ed. Elizabeth Maier and Nathalie Lebon (New Brunswick: Rutgers University Press, 2010), 60–75; Martha Nuñez Sarmiento, "A 'Top Down'–'Bottom Up' Model: Four Decades of Women's Employment and Gender Ideolog," in *Women's Activism in Latin America and the Caribbean*, ed. Elizabeth Maier and Nathalie Lebon (New Brunswick: Rutgers University Press, 2010), 76–91.

46 "Women interviewees admit that they educated their sons with macho patterns and trained their daughters to use their liberties carefully, for they live in a

highly machista society." Martha Nuñez Sarmiento, "A 'Top Down' – 'Bottom Up' Model: Four Decades of Women's Employment and Gender Ideolog," in *Women's Activism in Latin America and the Caribbean,* ed. Elizabeth Maier and Nathalie Lebon (New Brunswick: Rutgers University Press, 2010), 76–91.

47 "From these reflections I infer that men in my case studies are less prepared than women to act flexibly in terms of what it means to be man or woman in Cuba today. Men's ideology is less flexible than women's because they have been submitted to more indoctrination both as boys and adolescents. In general, they may ben as repressed as women, or even more so, in all spheres of life." Nuñez Sarmiento, Martha. "A 'Top Down' – 'Bottom Up' Model: Four Decades of Women's Employment and Gender Ideology." In Women's Activism in Latin America and the Caribbean, edited by Elizabeth Maier and Nathalie Lebon, New Brunswick: Rutgers University Press, 2010, p. 87.

48 "Long-standing policies intended to prioritize the needs of working mothers may thus be a burden for some women, constraining their choices and reinforcing their ties to a state sector that may offer symbolic capital in the form of social or political prestige, but yield little in the way of paid remuneration. [. . .] Despite this low overall workforce participation women hold over 70 percent of the state-sector jobs in education and health care, and also the majority in positions such as finance and insurance. While these state positions often require advanced qualifications, they are generally remunerated as part of the poorly paid peso economy." Elise Andaya, *Conceiving Cuba: Reproduction, Women and the State in Post-Soviet Era* (New Brunswick: Rutgers University Press, 2014), 108–9.

49 See not only Mala Htun and Juan Pablo Ossa, "Political Inclusion of Marginalized Groups: Indigenous Reservations and Gender Parity in Bolivia in Politics," *Politics, Groups and Identities* 1, no. 1 (2013): 4–25 and Toni Makkai, "Social Policy and Gender in Eastern Europe," in *Gendering Welfare State,* ed. Diane Sainsbury (Thousand Oaks: Sage Publications, 1994), 188–206, cited previously, but also Stéphanie Rousseau, "Indigenous and Feminist Movements at the Constituent Assembly in Bolivia: Locating the Representation of Indigenous Women," *Latin American Research Review* 46, no. 2 (2011): 5–28. Rousseau clearly states this fact in the following terms: "The contribution of the indigenous and feminist movements at the constituent assembly produced a very progressive constitution from the point of view of gender and ethnicity and from the point of view of specific indigenous women's claims," p. 6.

50 Bolivian Constitution (2009), Articles 8.II, 11.I, 14.II, 15.II, 26.I, 45.V, 48.VI, 66, 78.IV, 79, 147.I, 210.II, 395; Oscar Gonzalo Barrientos Jimenez, "Joint Democracy in Latin America: The de Jure and de Facto Situation of the Political Participation of Women in the Bolivian Context," *Revista Derecho del Estado* 40 (2018): 87–112:

"The Bolivian Constitution contains an important list of articles on participation and citizenship for women. Thus, article 11 states: 'The Republic of Bolivia adopts for its government the participatory, representative and communitarian democratic form, with equal conditions between men and women.' On the other hand, Article 26 states: 'All citizens have the right to participate freely in the formation, exercise and control of political power, directly or through their representatives, individually or collectively. Participation shall be equal and under the same conditions for men and women.' Articles 172.22 and 278.11 make explicit the participation in equivalence and equality of conditions between men and women, in the formation of the ministerial cabinet and the departmental assemblies, which opens the way to parity and gender alternation. Supreme

Decree 29894, dated February 7, 2009, establishes the organizational structure of the Executive Branch of the Plurinational State, and in its article 14.1.12 it incorporates the participation of women as servants in all state institutions.

Law 4021 on the Transitional Electoral System, of 14 April 2009; Law 018 on the Electoral Body, of 16 June 2010, and Law 026 on the Electoral System, of 30 June 2010, incorporate the constitutional principles of inclusion, non-discrimination, equal opportunities, gender equity, equivalence, parity and alternation in women's political participation. Article 2, paragraphs e and h of the Electoral Regime Law, orders the equality and equivalence of mandatory observance among the principles governing the exercise of intercultural democracy. In addition, it recognizes in Article 4 the equivalence of conditions between women and men for the exercise of political rights. Article 11 guarantees the equivalence of conditions, and obliges the authorities to guarantee and fulfill gender equity and equal opportunities between women and men, based on the criteria of alternation and parity. Likewise, it establishes that in the lists of candidates for senators, deputies, departmental and regional assemblies, municipal councilmen and other elected authorities, it will be guaranteed that there will be a female candidate and then a male candidate; a male substitute candidate and then a female substitute candidate, successively." Author's translation, pp. 96–97; additional to the articles in the constitution, in the Bolivian legal framework one may find the following laws related to women rights: Comprehensive Law to Guarantee Women a Free Life of Violence, Law Against Harassment and Political Violence Against Women, Comprehensive Law against Trafficking and Smuggling of Persons, Law Against Racism and All Forms of Discrimination, Social Control and Citizen Participation Law.

Bibliography

Alviar Garcia, Helena. *Engulfed by the Family: Women in the Colombian Development State between 1966 and 1990,* Rev. direito GV [online] 11, no. 2 (2015): 365–390.

Alviar Garcia, Helena. "Legal Reform, Social Policy, and Gendered Restribution in Columbia: The Role of the Family." *American University Journal of Gender Social Policy* (2011): 577–99.

Alviar Garcia, Helena. "Violence against Women as an Economic Issue: Making Sense of a Fragmented Field." *Brazilian Journal of Empirical Legal Studies* (2016): 53–72.

Andaya, Elise. *Conceiving Cuba: Reproduction, Women and the State in Post-Soviet Era.* New Brunswick: Rutgers University Press, 2014.

Barrientos Jimenez, Oscar Gonzalo. "Joint Democracy in Latin America: The de Jure and de Facto Situation of the Political Participation of Women in the Bolivian Context." *Revista Derecho del Estado* (2018): 87–112.

Beneria, Lourdes, and Gita Sen. "Accumulation, Reproduction, and 'Women's Role in Economic Development': Boserup Revisited." *Signs* (1982): 162–294.

Boserup, Ester. *Women's Role in Economic Development.* New York: St. Martin Press, 1970.

Castro, Fidel. "Discurso Pronunciado por Fidel Castro Ruíz, Presidente de la República de Cuba, En La Clausura de la V Plenaria Nacional de la FMC." *Año de la Solidaridad*. Santa Clara Las Villas, 1966. www.cuba.cu/gobierno/discursos/1966/esp/f091266e.html.

de Beauvoir, Simone. *The Second Sex*. New York: Vintage Books, 1973.

Deere, Carmen Diana, Helen Safa, and Peggy Antrobus. "Impact of the Economic Crisis on Poor Women and their Households." In *The Women, Gender and Development Reader*, edited by Nalini Visvanathan, Lynn Duggan, Laurie Nisonoff and Nan Wiegersma, 267–77. Zen Books, 1997.

Elson, Diane, and Ruth Pearson. "The Subordination of Women and the Internationalization of Factory Production." In *The Women, Gender and Development Reader*, edited by Nilini Visvanathan, Lynn Duggan, Laurie Nisonnof and Jan Wiegersma, 191–203. London: Zen Books, 1997.

Engels, Friedrich. "The Origin of the Family, Private Property and State." In *The Marx-Engels Reader*, edited by Robert C. Tucke, 744. New York: Norton, 1978.

Ferrante, Elena. *The Lost Daughter*. New York: Europa Editions, 2016.

Folbre, Nancy, Barbara Bergmann, and Maria Floro. *Issues in Contemporary Economics, Vol 4: Women's Work in the World Economy*. New York: New York University Press, 1992.

Goven, Joanna. "Sexual Politics in Hungary: Autonomy and Antifeminism." In *Sexual Politics and the Public Sphere: Women in Eastern Europe after the Transition*. London: Routledge, 1992.

Hidalgo Capitan, Antonio Luis, and Cubillo-Guevara, Ana Patricia. "Deconstruction and Genealogy of Latin American Good Living (Buen Vivir): The (Triune) Good Living and its Diverse Intellectual Wellsprings in Gilles Carbonnier." In *Alternative Pathways to Sustainable Development: Lessons from Latin America*, edited by Humberto Campodonico and Sergio Tenazos Vasquez, 24–37. Leiden: Brill, 2017.

Htun, Mala, and Juan Pablo Ossa. "Political Inclusion of Marginalized Groups: Indigenous Reservations and Gender Parity in Bolivia in Politics." *Politics, Groups and Identities*, 1, no. 1 (2013): 4–25.

Makkai, Toni. "Social Policy and Gender in Eastern Europe." In *Gendering Welfare State*, edited by Diane Sainsbury, 188–206. Thousand Oaks: Sage Publications, 1994.

Meurs, Mieke. "Downwardly Mobile: Women in the Decollectivization of East European Agriculture." In *The Women, Gender and Development Reader*, edited by Nalini Visvanathan, Lynn Duggn, Laurie Nisonoff and Nan Wiegersma, 333. London: Zen Books, 1997.

Murphy, Julieth S, Ofelia Schutte, Jan Slagter, and Linda Lopez McAlister. *Feminism in Cuba: Report from the Third Conference of North American and Cuban Philosphers*, 227–32. Hoboken: Hypatia, 1991.

Nuñez Sarmiento, Martha. "A 'Top Down'-'Bottom Up' Model: Four Decades of Women's Employment and Gender Ideology." In *Women's Activism in Latin America and the Caribbean*, edited by Elizabeth Maier and Nathalie Lebon, 76–91. New Brunswick: Rutgers University Press, 2010.

Revista Semana. "El polémico video de Alejandro Ordóñez sobre la ideología de género y la paz." *Revista Semana*, September 2016.

Rostow, W. W. "The Stages of Economic Growth: A Non-Communist Manifesto (1960)." In *The Globalization and Development Reader: Perspectives on Development and Global Change*, edited by Timmons Roberts, Amy Bellone Hite and Nitsan Chorev, 52. Hoboken: Wiley-Blackwell, 2015.

Rousseau, Stéphanie. "Indigenous and Feminist Movements at the Constituent Assembly in Bolivia: Locating the Representation of Indigenous Women." *Latin American Research Review* (2011): 5–28.

Safa, Helen. "Female Headed Households and Poverty in Latin America: A Comparison of Cuba, Puerto Rico, and the Dominican Republic." In *Women's Activism in Latin America and the Caribbean*, edited by Elizabeth Maier and Nathalie Lebon, 60–75. New Brunswick: Rutgers University Press, 2010.

Said, Edward. "Orientalism." In *The Post-Colonial Studies Reader*, edited by Bill Ashcroft, Gareth Griffiths and Helen Tiffin, 88–89. London: Routledge, 1997.

Tinker, Irene. "The Making of a Field: Advocates, Practitioners and Scholars." In *The Women Gender and Development Reader*, edited by T Nlini Visvanathan, Lynn Dugan, Laurie Nisonoff and Nan Wiegerma. London: Zed books, 1997.

4   Social policy and economic development

Inseparable

As I write this, in September of 2020, the tools that governments in the region have set forth to face Covid-19 continue to be elusive and evocative of the plague of insomnia powerfully described by Gabriel García Márquez in *One Hundred Years of Solitude*:

> When Jose Arcadio Buendia realized that the plague had invaded the town, he gathered together the heads of families to explain to them what he knew about the sickness of insomnia, and they agreed on methods to prevent the scourge from spreading to other towns in the swamp. That was why they took bells off the goats, bells that the Arabs had swapped for macaws, and put them at the entrance to town at the disposal of those who would not listen to the advice and entreaties of the sentinels and insisted on visiting the town. All strangers who passed through the streets of Macondo at that time had to ring their bells so that the sick people would know that they were healthy. They were not allowed to eat or drink anything during their stay, for there was no doubt that the illness was transmitted by mouth, and all food and drink had been contaminated by insomnia. In that way they kept the plague restricted to the perimeter of town. So effective was the quarantine that the day came when the emergency situation was accepted as a natural thing and life was organized in such a way that work picked up its rhythm again and no one worried any more about the useless habit of sleeping.
>
> (García Márquez 2006)

The quote speaks so much to the Covid-19 crisis. Then, as now, the instruments available to prevent it were lockdowns to contain its spread, fear of strangers and the eventual incorporation of the virus as a natural way of life. Despite the similar historical patterns, when the pandemic hit the region in early March, many Latin American countries were restricted by neoliberal policies in the economic and social sphere. This chapter aims to explore some of the conditions that framed government choices when handling the pandemic. It proposes that export-led growth combined with neoliberal social policy design has left the region ill equipped to face a crisis of this magnitude. The interaction between economic development goals and social policies has greatly limited the scope and breadth of welfare provisions. In fact, distributing social services for the population does not happen in a vacuum, it is determined by ideas about growth, the role of the state and the prevalence of the market.

The text starts out with an overview of the interaction between economic development and social policy. Then, it analyzes the central characteristics of neoliberalism set in relation to welfare style provisions: the dismantling of state intervention, health privatization and the centrality of conditional cash transfers. This is followed by an outline of the style of policies designed by the Cuban government as a counterpoint and an example of a universalistic approach to social services. It is not the aim of the chapter to defend the Cuban model; much has been written about the dire conditions in which its population lives and the inequality that characterizes it. Instead, Cuban social policies are brought as an opposite model, even if in paper. The descriptions of the different countries presented are not comprehensive; they are included to illustrate examples of choices taken by neoliberal governments as well as those that have more universal, centralized state welfare provisions. The text ends with a discussion of how the Covid-19 crisis affected Latin American countries that relied on neoliberalism in the form of export-led growth as the basic economic development model along with conditional cash transfers and a privatized health system as essential welfare tools.

General background

A welfare state is a state in which organized power is deliberately used (through politics and administration) in an effort to modify the play of market forces in at least three directions: first, by guaranteeing individuals and families a minimum of income irrespective of the market value of their work or their property; second, by narrowing the extent of insecurity by enabling individuals and families to meet certain social contingencies (for example, sickness, old age and unemployment) which lead otherwise to individual and family crises; and third, by ensuring that all citizens without distinction of status or class are offered the best standards available in relation to a certain agreed range of social services.

.   (Briggs 2006)

In this classical definition of the welfare state, historian Asa Briggs describes the duties that this style of government encapsulates. Importantly, protecting individuals from the whims of capitalism by making sure that citizens and their families earn a minimum amount of resources that does not depend upon how much they work, the job they have or the property they own. In addition, both individuals and their families should be aided when faced with events such as sickness, work-related injuries, disability, maternity, childbearing, unemployment, retirement or death and they should be guaranteed access to specific goods such as electricity, heat and water.

This generous undertaking was never the rule in Latin America. As a matter of fact, during the postwar years and before the neoliberal wave, most countries linked social insurance and health provision to the male breadwinner, leaving behind women (Alviar, Legal Reform, Social Policy, and Gendered Redistribution in Colombia: The Role of the Family 2011), informal as well as rural workers. Of course, there were differences. In countries such as Uruguay, Chile, Costa Rica and Argentina, people have had at times far-reaching benefits in comparison to people in Peru, Colombia and Mexico.[1]

One of the main arguments of this chapter is that welfare-style policies are unintelligible without a consideration to their relationship to economic development models, that there is a dynamic relationship between the processes of economic transformation and the design of welfare promotion interventions, along with the legal tools that are available. In this sense, if the definition of development is growth by import substitution industrialization, the provision of social services will most likely be linked to full employment, and therefore the basic tool to distribute resources within society will be a minimum wage, social security and family subsidies for formal workers. Public law is central to this model, mostly in the form of administrative regulations, including tariffs to defend local industries along with the centrality of labor law to protect formal workers and their families.

On the other hand, if the definition of economic development is export-led growth and a belief that the market is the adequate distributor of resources, social provisions will be designed in order to enable access to the market. Citizens must be able to buy health, contribute to private pension funds and pay for water, electricity or other services that are provided by private corporations. In the cases that the trickle-down effects of growth do not reach portions of the population, individual, needs-based conditional cash transfers are the preferred social policy. This restriction of the domain of social policy has as a consequence the changing understanding of poverty and poverty alleviation. This shift goes from a macro/structural phenomenon that should be addressed through development policy goals and macroeconomic policy instruments to a localized phenomenon focused on individual/ household fortunes that should be addressed by individuals adjudicating entitlements on the basis of the constitutional bill of rights, and conditional cash transfers to households on a means-test basis. For this market-led

Table 4.1 Summary of economic development idea

Economic Development Idea	Idea of Social Policy	Role of the State	Law
ISI	SP is a tool; increase demand for locally produced goods through formal worker protection	Defend and promote local industries; promote full employment and guarantee formal workers' rights	Public law, labor law and administrative law
Dependency	SP is a tool to redistribute resources; universal health care, access to essential services such as health, education, sanitation, electricity	State-led growth and state provision of public services	Public law: constitutional and executive orders
Market-Oriented Reforms	SP is a tool to help people enter the market; conditional cash transfers	Minimal state Macro-economic stability; market as best resource allocator	Private law: contracts, corporate and competition law, protection of private property

model, private law in the form of contracts, corporate and competition law and the protection of private property became central.

In addition, if the definition of economic development is nationalized, state-led growth (export of a single product such as sugar in the initial stages of Cuba, oil in the case of Venezuela and hydrocarbons in the case of Bolivia) social policy design will be universal access and redistribution of resources across class lines, through constitutional law, labor rights and executive orders.

Table 4.1 summarizes these ideas.

Setting the stage for the difficulties faced by neoliberal states in Latin America

Dismantling state intervention

For the last 30 years, Latin American countries have been told again and again that a minimal state is the key to economic development by neoliberal academics and policy makers. This critique of government intervention was set forth, among others, by P.T. Bauer, who famously stated: "Nations are not poor because they are poor, that is, because of vicious circles; rather they are poor because of too much government interference" (Cypher and Dietz 1997).[2] The dismantling of government interference was based upon three basic ideas: the public sector has become too fundamental for the economies in the Third World; governments had concentrated too much on big investment projects; and state intervention (in the form of subsidies or public service provision, for example) created price distortions, picked winners and unduly benefitted certain areas of the economy. In addition, all of this government presence required high levels of spending, which in turn was translated into budget deficits and high inflation rates.

In sum, neoliberalism in Latin America was crystallized in the elimination of welfare style policies (that were replaced by conditional cash transfers), the privatization of social service provision and the reduction of state investment in certain areas of the economy. From the late 1980s through the late 1990s, many workers' benefits were eliminated and direct state investment in health and education was diminished.

The minimal state had three manifestations that deeply affected the tools available for governments during the pandemic: the elimination or weakening of publicly funded and administered social services (such as education and health care) and its transfer to private entities, the diminishment of state spending along with an obsession with austerity and the replacement of welfare style policies and bureaucracies with conditional cash transfers.

The arguments for relinquishing government intervention in favor of market forces had their origins in critiques aimed at the harms brought by state intervention in the region. Neoliberal theory in Latin America interpreted government not as the ultimate manifestation of the social good, but as a set of individuals carving out space for their self-interested agendas. Therefore, when governments deployed their power by owning a steel mill, a car factory, a hotel business; protecting infant industries or subsidizing health care, water and fuel, they were distorting prices and choosing winners. Officials who managed public resources or were in charge of regulation were motivated by self-interest and found rent-seeking opportunities at every turn. These interventions are detrimental to the market, inefficient and therefore should be avoided at all costs. In sum, governments should refrain from interfering, otherwise they will distort market prices, privilege some areas of the economy over others and open the door for corruption.

In terms of public spending, many governments in the region were convinced that austerity was essential. According to neoliberal theory, public spending distorts prices, contributes to inflation and interferes with private investment. As stated earlier, government subsidies on basic goods such as food staples, milk, meat, health care services and pharmaceutical products should be eliminated. In his fascinating account regarding the evolution of the term "austerity," economist Mark Blyth summarizes its justification in the following terms:

> Austerity is a form of voluntary deflation in which the economy adjusts through the reduction of wages, prices and public spending to restore competitiveness, which is (supposedly) best achieved by cutting the state's budget, debts and deficits. In doing so, its advocates believe, will inspire "business confidence" since the government will neither be "crowding out" the market for investment by sucking up all the available capital through the issuance of debt, nor adding to the nation's already "too big" debt.
>
> (Blyth 2013)

On the other hand, the moral argument behind forcing states to embrace austerity appears to be as strong as neoliberal justifications for it:

> In terms of how we think about austerity today, Smith's moral critique of debt seems as familiar as Hume's economic one. Saving is a virtue, spending is a vice. Countries that save must be doing the right thing, while spenders must be storing up trouble.
>
> (Blyth 2013)

Reducing state spending had many consequences, among them drastic cuts on health services and infrastructure, a withdrawal from universal coverage, privatization of previously state-provided services[3] and the granting of public funds for health to private corporations whose driving force is profit.[4]

Health privatization

Privatization of health is strong in Latin America (Giovanella and Faria 2015). Reforms led in Chile and Colombia are striking examples of this move toward understanding health provision as a private, corporate activity instead of a universal right. Neoliberal health policy assumes that corporations are better equipped to efficiently manage medical services.[5] This managerial approach includes evaluating services through the cost-effective lens that the World Bank strongly promoted in 1993:

> When governments become directly involved in the health sector – by providing public health programs or financing essential clinical services for the poor – policymakers face difficult decisions concerning

the allocation of public resources. For any given amount of total spending, taxpayers and, in some countries, donors want to see maximum health gain for the money they spent.

(Berkley et al. 1993)

Along the same neoliberal governance lines, the multilateral institution promotes "performance-based incentives for managers and clinicians, and related training and development of management systems" (Berkley et al. 1993). As if following a script, the Bank's formula for improving access to health care includes increasing growth in order to reduce poverty; decreasing the amount of public resources used on less cost-effective interventions and "foster competition and diversity in the supply of health services and inputs, particularly drugs, supplies and equipment" (Berkley et al. 1993). An additional detrimental consequence of granting health care services to private corporations is that administrative expenses go up. These costs are used to pay for "marketing, billing, denial of claims, processing copayments and deductibles, exorbitant salaries and deferred income for executives, profits and dividends for corporate shareholders" (Waitzkin and Hellander, Obamacare: The Neoliberal Model Comes Home to Roost in the United States – If We Let It 2018).

Chile, for example, underwent a market-oriented health reform whose main objective was to lower the fiscal deficit by reducing social expenditure and privatizing the social security system (Giovanella and Faria 2015). One of the most significant characteristics of this reform is that it established the stratification of health care: people with higher incomes would select their insurance from what the market offered, people with middle-income could access private health insurance through co-payments depending on their incomes and people with low incomes would have access to health care from state services with a proof of poverty (Giovanella and Faria 2015). Under this reform, the country also began to decentralize its publicly provided health services, establishing 26 health services areas to cover 13 different administrative regions (Berkley et al. 1993). From the state's point of view, its intervention would strengthen competition and boost the market dynamics; and according to the World Bank Report of 1993, policies that increased the efficiency of government health services through decentralization and strengthened competition of the private sector were considered desirable (Berkley et al. 1993). The positive results have yet to be seen, and according to research advanced in 2015, the development of a private insurance system and the privatization of services in Chile increased the levels of inequality regarding coverage and access to health care (Giovanella and Faria 2015).

Colombia has followed a similar path. In 1993, under Cesar Gaviria's government and highly influenced by the World Bank recommendations (Esteves 2012), Colombia's market-oriented reform took place. With Law

100 of 1993, the administration wanted to address two different issues: the funding crisis of the public, social security institute due to the high levels of spending in health, along with the aim of implementing universal health care coverage (Vargas and Méndez 2014).

The idea was to foster competition of both public and private sectors and to provide a middle ground between opposing ideas about how health care should be provided: through privatization or through state national services (Giovanella and Faria 2015). Decentralization was also an important element of the reform and a state institution (*Superintendencia de Salud*) would be in charge of regulation and supervision. Providing health care was transferred to both private and public organizations, but after a few years private entities prevailed (Giovanella and Faria 2015). Nevertheless, the problems following the implementation of Law 100 of 1993 and a market-based transformation were significant in terms of equity, efficiency, quality and high corruption levels (Abadía-Barrero 2016). Due to funding problems and inefficient administration, public hospitals were at a disadvantage compared to private operators, and today most of the distribution of health care services has been privatized (Esteves 2012). In a vast number of cases, private health care providers have denied services, treatments and medications, forcing people to fight for their right to access health care in court. From 1999 to 2012, the judicial system received more than one million *tutelas* (Abadía-Barrero 2016): a tool for the protection of constitutional rights – such as the right to health.

The centrality of conditional cash transfers

Since 1997 and up to now, countries all across the political spectrum in Latin America have adopted conditional cash transfers. As a matter of fact, during the initial years of the twenty-first century, most countries had this style of policy (Borges 2018). Research published in 2018 established that 25% of Latin America's population was covered by conditional cash transfers.[6] According to some accounts, it has been described as reducing poverty levels by 13% as well as diminishing income inequality and improving school enrollment (Borges 2018).

Conditional cash transfers are designed to reach the poorest households that are subject to the verification of the fulfillment of certain commitments such as attending school, health checkups, supervising the gaining of weight of children and in some cases looking for a job. Examples of these initiatives are *Progresa/Oportunidades* in Mexico, *Bolsa Escola/Bolsa Familia* in Brazil, *Trabajar/Jefes y Jefas de Hogar* in Argentina and *Familias en Acción* in Colombia. They were at times combined with other anti-poverty programs such as direct grants that did not depend on any duty, such as *Fome Cero* in Brazil or integrated policies in Chile *Solidario*.[7]

The amount of resources that each household receives varies across countries, but it is designed to act as a supplement, not a replacement of income, as they are geared specifically to aid in access to health, education and nutrition. The transfers are supposed to be regular, reliable and last for a rather long period of time (although most programs include a termination or graduation term, as when children reach a certain age or members of the household get a job). Many programs are designed to combine other services such as providing resources for school uniforms and books or replacing earnings from children's work when they go to school (Barrientos and Santibáñez 2009).

Conditional cash transfers have very specific selection methods that include geographical criteria, means tests, proxy means tests (an estimation of the household income when it is unavailable, or it is a challenge to obtain)[8] and community participation. These selection methods are not only aimed at excluding those who don't need assistance but also generating a scale of household poverty (Barrientos and Santibáñez 2009). Resources are delivered in many forms and are set forth by the offices of Health and Education or the Ministry of Planning (Barrientos and Santibáñez 2009).[9]

Despite the widespread use of this style of program, ideological differences account for the depth and breadth of these programs, as I have argued in previous work:

> I propose that the adoption of new social policies, even if consistent with regional best practices, does not necessarily co-relate with positive developmental outcomes. More specifically, I argue that the success of new social policies is not only path dependent but also seems to be determined by two additional, interrelated factors. On the one hand, on the specific political choices and economic development models that made the adoptions of these policies possible. In this sense, conditional cash transfers adopted in the context of a political choice to reduce structural and historical inequality are incomparable to ones adopted as a measure to help families in moments of crisis, reduce the burden on the government's budget, treat poverty as a localized phenomenon ultimately linked to individual/household fortunes, or strengthened in order to enhance the political capital of a very powerful executive.
>
> (Alviar, Social Policy and the New Development State 2013)

An initial counterpoint, the welfare state in Cuba: universal provisions with financing difficulties

Cuban social policy is radically different from the means tested approach. In paper, at least, it starts out with principles of equity among all members of society, universal access, publicly funded services and all citizens entitled to welfare provisions. The benefits include food and housing subsidies; protection for workers' employment and unemployment benefits; access to social security, health and education (Uriarte-Gaston 2004). In 1961, the state decided to establish a nationally integrated public health care system with universal and free access, which also aimed to reduce substantial gaps between rural and urban areas in terms of facilities, personnel and service quality (Mesa-Lago 2017). In order to do this, the state expropriated all private health care facilities, cooperatives and mutual-aid societies, and prohibited the private practice of medicine (Mesa-Lago 2017). Nevertheless, this type of reform was very expensive, and initiatives such as the family doctor program created in 1984 demanded significant investment (Mesa-Lago 2017). In spite of its costs, and as Mesa-Lago describes, the health care reforms were very successful:

> The revolution's health care system policy was quite successful during its first three decades. In 1959 till 1989 the ratio of physicians increased from 9.2 to 33 per 10,000 inhabitants, hospital beds from 4.2 to 5.1 per 1,000 inhabitants, and real expenditures per habitant by 162 percent. Infant mortality decreased from 33.4 to 11.1 per 1,000 children born alive, maternal mortality shrank from 125.3 to 29.2 per 100,000 births, and mortality of the population aged 65 and above declined from 52.9 to 46.3 for 1,000 in this age group. Most contagious diseases were eliminated, but the incidence of chickenpox, sexually transmitted diseases including aids and hepatitis, as well as diarrheic and acute respiratory diseases increased.
>
> (Mesa-Lago 2017)

Despite a crisis during the 1990s after the fall of the Soviet Union and the Eastern European countries, the commitment to universal access to welfare benefits continued (Uriarte-Gaston 2004).[10] Notwithstanding these commitments and after 1993 when the government opened the country to foreign investment and a dual monetary system, inequality in Cuba has increased significantly. Given the fact that the average Cuban salary is around 30 US dollars (Hansing and Hoffmann 2019), access to resources beyond state salaries has made the difference in equality levels in the country. Complementing employment income comes mostly from two sources: remittances and small, private market activities either informal or legal self-employment. Having the capacity to tap into this type of additional funds is hardly distributed equally among Cuban citizens. According to some research, black Cubans have far less access to additional sources of income (Hansing and Hoffmann 2019),[11] and, as a consequence, they are poorer and don't have a banking account or access to the Internet (Hansing and Hoffmann 2019).[12] Despite an increase in inequality, state provision of social services continues to be strong:

> Monetary income is not the only factor defining material status, particularly in a socialist country like Cuba, where state subsidies are prevalent. Cuba's welfare provisions have largely been non-monetary, and although their quality and scope have eroded over time, they still need to be taken into account. As such, despite major cutbacks the food rationing system still distributes basic food supplies at almost symbolic CUP prices. Education and healthcare are free, and public transportation as well as arts/cultural and sports are heavily subsidized. Also, given that most Cubans own their own home and rents are subsidized, housing costs are not as central a concern as elsewhere.
>
> (Hansing and Hoffmann 2019)

The Covid-19 crisis: neoliberal governance failing at the task

Covid-19 has had and will have particular economic, social and political effects according to the prevailing characteristics of the place it hits. Along with the specific attributes a country may have, one of the most puzzling aspects of the illness has been how it affects even neighboring places disparately. According to the *New York Times*, this is the case of Iran being devastated by it and Iraq having only 100 deaths, and the Dominican Republic where there are more than 8,000 cases while neighboring Haiti has fewer than 90 (Beech et al. 2020), among a few other remarkable cases. Despite the dissimilarities in the devastation (and according to the article, this could be just a product of lack of testing capacities or an issue of time), public policy design varies according to national and regional features and, this chapter argues, is determinant in structuring the possibilities of success.

As the pandemic has ravaged the continent, national economic growth has been stalled after decades of centering it on export-led growth. As Dependency theorists predicted more than 60 years ago, the fact that Latin American economies are mostly concentrated on the production and export of primary products makes them acutely vulnerable to the luck of the Global North. The Economic Commission for Latin America and the Caribbean, in a report regarding the effects of Covid-19, describes five reasons why the region is particularly ill equipped:

> the decline in the economic activity of the region's main trading partners; the drop in commodity prices; the interruption of global value

chains; the lower demand for tourism services and the greater risk aversion and worsening of global financial conditions.

(ECLAC 2020a)

In addition, policies available to increase state spending were structurally limited after more than 30 years of fiscal discipline and an obsession over curtailing inflation (Blackman et al. 2020).[13]

In line with the overarching argument of this chapter, economic, social policies and their pairing legal instruments are not created or set forth in a vacuum. Covid-19 proves that the possibilities for their initial design and their subsequent impact are determined by the specific political, economic and social characteristics a country had before the crisis. These limits can also be predicated about the tool box of legal challenges available to lawyers and citizens interested in counterbalancing authoritarianism or voicing concerns about its surge. In Latin America, most of the pushback has come from human rights organizations arguing a disproportionate curtailment of freedoms and a lack of an adequate checks and balances.[14] Not much debate surrounded the concentration of economic relief for big companies (in a region where 99% of them are small and medium size) (ECLAC 2020a), the difficulties of protecting formal workers – many of whom have stopped receiving their whole salary or part of it (ECLAC 2020b) – and the restrictions a neoliberal state faces when trying to reach great swaths of informal workers: many of these workers do not have enough savings to face the crisis, social distancing measures prevent them from pursuing their activities and generating income, and most of them can barely access unemployment insurance or health care (ECLAC 2020b).

As stated earlier, when the pandemic struck, 25% of Latin America's population received most of its welfare provisions through conditional cash transfers. This meant that they only way that weak, dismantled states could reach citizens in need was through conditional cash transfer recipients that had been previously identified through official social registries (López-Calva 2020). This, of course, brought as a consequence that many remained hidden because they were not vulnerable before the crisis or because they were not part of official records to start with. In a UNDP report, these are called the "missing middle" and "hidden poor":

> In some countries, social registries cover a far broader segment of the population than those currently receiving cash transfers (suggesting vast scope for rapid horizontal expansion of benefits) . . . it is also critical that countries expand coverage of social registries to both include the "missing middle" as well as to ensure that extra efforts are made to include the "hidden poor." The "missing middle" refers to groups such as vulnerable households or informal workers that may not have

been "poor" prior to the pandemic but may now be eligible for social assistance benefits.

(López-Calva 2020)

Taking stock of the policies to confront the pandemic

In the birthplace of magical realism, there has been some of it, represented mostly by Bolsonaro in Brazil, Ortega in Nicaragua and AMLO in Mexico. Bolsonaro, for example, in response to deaths rising, said: "So what? I'm sorry, what do you want me to do?" (Phillips 2020). He has described the virus as a little flu, joined protests against lockdown, coughed in public without protection, claimed Brazilian people are particularly strong and do not get the virus and demanded that the sickness should be faced like a man, not a boy. On July 7th, 2020, President Bolsonaro tested positive for Covid-19 (Londoño, Andreoni, and Casado 2020). In Nicaragua, Daniel Ortega organized a march under the slogan "Love in the times of COVID-19" and AMLO has taken prayer cards out of his wallet, claiming these images along with his personal honesty have protected him against the virus (Agren 2020).

Most governments passed social distancing orders, health-strengthening policies and economic crisis management decrees. As it has happened elsewhere in the world, there are differences in terms of how quickly the lockdown happened, how strict it was, the areas it covered and the penalties for not abiding (Malamud and Núñez 2020).

The strict measures regarding social distancing and restriction of movement are leading to job losses (11.6 million more unemployed in 2020, compared to 2019) and reducing personal and household income (ECLAC 2020b). Trends in poverty and extreme poverty will also be affected: in 2020, poverty in Latin America may rise by at least 4.4 percentage points (28.7 million more people) compared to 2019, and extreme poverty is likely to increase by 2.6 percentage points (15.9 million more people), affecting a total of 83.4 million (ECLAC 2020b). Another important field that will continue to be affected is education and other variables linked to it. The suspension of classes not only makes it impossible to attend school – as of March 2020, 154 million children and teenagers were temporarily out of school due to the pandemic (ECLAC 2020a) – but it also impacts other elements such as care, parent's participation in the market and nutrition – 85 million children in Latin America are being fed at school (either breakfast, snack or lunch) (ECLAC 2020a). Unemployment is also expected to increase and, due to the social and economic inequalities in the region, its effects will disproportionately affect the poor (ECLAC 2020a).

The measures to counteract the effects of the pandemic were heralded as an enormous increase in the levels of state spending to aid the poor. The truth is that neoliberal governance continues to frame the options available. In the following paragraphs, two examples of the structural limitations imposed by neoliberalism will be analyzed: the minimal state as exemplified by the privatization of health care and the expansion of conditional cash transfers instead of state-centered welfare policies.

In relation to health privatization and as mentioned earlier, even before the pandemic, access to health was unequal and inefficient. Despite its disheartening performance, health privatization was mostly left in place with little reform, and, today, most of the distribution of health care services in the region has been privatized (Esteves 2012). This isn't unique to Latin America, of course; research advanced by UNDP in 2019 and WHO 2020, clearly established that in 147 countries there is a "positive relationship between private health-care provision and health inequality" (Assa and Calderon 2020). In the same paper, the authors conclude that privatization does not prepare national health systems for a pandemic:

> The results presented above indicate that private spending on health care significantly raises the rates of COVID-19 prevalence and mortality across countries, controlling for their income, urbanization, demographic structure, exposure to globalization and political system. These findings add to the existing literature showing the inadequacy of private healthcare systems in addressing other infectious diseases such as TB.
> [. . .]
> Our findings suggest that, to make health systems sustainable at various levels of development and given the expectation of worsening environmental conditions, there is an urgent need to reconsider the neoliberal impulse to privatize health care systems. The short-term benefits from such privatization policies – e.g. reduced costs, shorter waiting times – must be weighed against the long-term damage such policies can do countries' ability to cope with a rapidly-spreading infectious disease.
>
> (Assa and Calderon 2020)

Cash transfers replacing the welfare state

As the first part of this chapter showed conditional cash transfers are pervasive in Latin America and that have mostly replaced broader, comprehensive social welfare state structures (United Nations 2020).[15] Argentina, for example, extended a policy to benefit informal workers through a payment of around 140 US dollars (Ministerio de Economía – Gobierno de Argentina 2020). Colombia increased cash transfer payments through the existing program, Familias en Acción (Gobierno de Colombia 2020). In Costa Rica, the Bono

Proteger allows a monthly transfer of 125,000 colones (US$ 220) for three months to informal and independent workers, as well as to people who have had their employment contracts suspended or their working hours reduced by more than half (ECLAC 2020b). As for Brazil, an emergency grant is being provided to independent or informal workers that have a monthly income of less than half the minimum wage and a household income of less than three times the minimum wage (ECLAC 2020b). In Chile, a 2 billion dollar fund was created in order to aid people with informal jobs through a family income support bonus (Ulloa 2020). Additional policies have been subsidies for wages, tax deferrals and the suspension of public service payments. In Argentina, a suspension of the precautionary measures corresponding to tax-payers registered in the "Registro de empresas MiPyMES" was set in place; in Chile, tax refunds that correspond to natural persons (dependent and inde-pendent workers) by way of income tax were established; and in Colombia, there was a Value Added Tax elimination for the import of products, articles and technologies for the health to address this situation.

In a region where precarious job conditions are the rule, confinement was tricky. As a matter of fact, and according to ECLAC data, 53% of workers in the region are in the informal sector (ECLAC 2020a), which explains the reluctance to place strict lockdown measures, as many need the streets for survival. In addition, because of ideas related to the minimal state, governments had little institutional capacity to forcefully set out welfare policies. As a consequence, many citizens are unreachable either because they are not beneficiaries of conditional cash transfers (they may have had slightly higher incomes before the pandemic) or they have informal jobs that exclude them from workers' benefits. Due to business closings, there will be rising unemployment numbers, and this will in turn have an impact on the resources of weak, existing social protection systems through the reduction of direct contributions (ECLAC 2020b).

A silver lining could be that Covid-19 has revived discussions regarding the establishment of a universal income as a way of social protection, some-thing unthinkable a few months before (El Espectador 2020).[16] Accord-ing to ECLAC recommendations, "social protection counteracts the loss of sources of labour income and supports demand by safeguarding house-hold income and consumption, while at the same time facilitating access to health" (ECLAC 2020b).

Conclusions

The goal of this chapter has been to argue that social policy design is not taken in a vacuum, rather it is directly related to the possibilities granted by economic development plans and the corresponding legal tools used to advance it. In addition, the text has demonstrated how the minimal state demanded by neoliberal ideals was manifested in two very particular ways that had dire consequences when facing Covid-19: health care privatization and the dismantling of welfare state provisions.

Health care privatization created a two-tier system where those who could buy insurance had access to differentiated quality and levels of service; hospitals that were ill prepared to face the pandemic because the sector was run as a business and not a public service. The dismantling of welfare provisions led to a weak institutional arrangement that was incapable of delivering social services to the many citizens in Latin America who were either fired from their jobs or had no access even to precarious, subsistence work.

Notes

1 For a comprehensive comparison on the development of welfare style policies in the region, see Stephan Haggard and Robert R. Kaufman, *Development, Democracy, and Welfare States: Latin America, East Asia, and Eastern Europe* (Princeton: Princeton University Press, 2008).
2 P.T. Bauer cited in James M. Cypher and James L. Dietz, *The Process of Economic Development* (New York: Routledge, 1997), 217.
3 For the effects of structural adjustment in Latin America see: Helena Alviar, *Derecho, desarrollo y feminismo en América Latina* (Bogotá: Universidad de los Andes, 2008).
4 For a fascinating analysis of the relationship between neoliberalism, capitalism and health see: Howard Waitzkin, *Health Care Under the Knife: Moving beyond Capitalism for Our Health* (New York: Monthly Review Press, 2018).
5 "An underlying managerial ideology claimed, nearly always without evidence, that corporate executives could achieve superior quality and efficiency by 'managing' medical services in the market place." Howard Waitzkin and Ida Hellander, "Obamacare: The Neoliberal Model Comes Home to Roost in the United States – If We Let It," in *Health Care under the Knife: Moving Beyond Capitalism for Our Health*, ed. Howard Waitzkin (New York: Monthly Review Press, 2018), 104.
6 This number is probably higher as a result of Covid-19.
7 For a complete list, see Enrique Valencia, "Conditional Cash Transfers as Social Policy in Latin America: An Assessment of their Contributions and Limitations," *Annual Review of Sociology* 34 (2008): 475–98.
8 For more on this methodology, see https://olc.worldbank.org/sites/default/files/1.pdf.
9 "Chile Solidario Works through a consolidated Budget, incorporating the budgets of its associated programmes, under the coordination of the Ministry of Planning. The annual Budget legislation allocates resources to the Ministry of Planning, which in turn negotiates allocations to the final executing agencies through formal contracts. Colombia's Familias en Acción, opted to allocate resources directly to the executing agencies, while specifically the destination and use of the resources in the annual Budget legislation. In Brazil, Chile and Colombia, municipalities coordinate many áreas of program implementation.

In Mexico and Panama, programme implementation is centralised. The point is to ensure financial and economic efficiency through authorised and effective institutional practices," p. 23.

10 "by the end of the decade, it was evident that the principal elements of Cuban social policy had remained in place. Cuba did not seek efficiencies through privatization, nor did it seek to redefine its responsibility for the provisions of social benefits," p. 107.

11 "When asked why they didn't receive remittances, 85% of Afro-Cubans responded that they did not have family abroad, while among whites this was the case for only 28%." Hansing and Hoffman, p. 15. "The self-employed make up 8.6 percent of whites versus 6.4 percent of blacks and 6.6 percent of mulattoes." p. 19.

12 "Among Afro-Cubans, 70 percent responded that they had no internet access whatsoever; among whites this was down 25 per cent. Almost two thirds of White Cubans do have access via public áreas such as the Wi-Fi zones in public parks; for Afro-Cubans this a mere 28 percent," p. 12.

13 According to the Inter-American Development Bank's public policy recommendations for Latin America, "[g]iven the current debt levels, and taking into account the relationship between the level of debt and the fiscal expansion [. . .], the response capacity today would be, on average, approximately half, or 1.5 percent of GDP."

14 See among others: Roberto Gargarella, "The Fight against COVID-19 in Argentina: Executive vs Legislative Branch," May 1, 2020, https://verfassungsblog. de/the-fight-against-covid-19-in-argentina-executive-vs-legislative-branch/; Esteban Hoyos-Ceballos and Julián Gaviria-Mira, "Pandemic and Executive Powers in Colombia: A Problem and a Modest Proposal," April 17, 2020, https:// verfassungsblog.de/pandemic-and-executive-powers-in-colombia-a-problem-and-a-modest-proposal/; Aaron Alfredo Acosta, Nelson Camilo Sánchez León, and Mohammad Zia, "Confronting COVID-19 in Colombia," June 18, 2020, www.dejusticia.org/en/publication/confronting-covid-19-in-colombia/.

15 According to the United Nations Policy Brief on The Impact of COVID-19 on Latin America and the Caribbean "[t]he cash and in-kind transfers implemented in 26 countries to support families in situations of poverty and vulnerability during the crisis covered approximately 69 million households (286 million people, or 44% of the population)," www.un.org/sites/un2.un.org/files/sg_policy_brief_covid_lac.pdf.

16 In Colombia, for example, not only one but four drafts of legal bills were being discussed in July of 2020. For more on this, see El Espectador, "Cuatro proyectos que abren el debate sobre la renta básica universal en Colombia," *El Espectador*, July 28, 2020, www.elespectador.com/noticias/politica/renta-basica-universal-en-colombia-cuatro-proyectos-de-ley-que-abren-el-debate/.

Bibliography

Abadía-Barrero, César Ernesto. "Neoliberal Justice and the Transformation of the Moral: The Privatization of the Right to Health Care in Colombia." *Medical Anthropology Quarterly* 30, no. 1 (March 2016): 62–79.

Acosta, Aaron Alfredo, Nelson Camilo Sánchez León, and Mohammad Zia. "Confronting COVID-19 in Colombia," June 18, 2020. www.dejusticia.org/en/publication/confronting-covid-19-in-colombia/.

Agren, David. "Mexico's López Obrador Holds Daily Briefings Rivalling Trump's: 'A Spectacle without any Value.'" *The Guardian*, May 4, 2020. www.theguardian.com/world/2020/may/04/mexico-president-amlo-coronavirus-briefings-like-trump.

Alviar, Helena. *Derecho, desarrollo y feminismo en América Latina*. Bogotá: Universidad de los Andes, 2008.

Alviar, Helena. "Legal Reform, Social Policy, and Gendered Redistribution in Colombia: The Role of the Family." *American University Journal of Gender Social Policy and Law* 19, no. 2 (2011): 577–99.

Alviar, Helena. "Social Policy and the New Development State." In *Law and the New Developmental State: The Brazilian Experience in Latin American Context*, edited by David M. Trubek, Helena Alviar, Diogo R. Coutinho and Alvaro Santos. Cambridge: Cambridge University Press, 2013.

Assa, Jacob, and Maria Cecilia Calderon. "Privatization and Pandemic: A Cross-Country Analysis of COVID-19 Rates and Health-Care Financing Structures." *ResearchGate*, May 2020. www.researchgate.net/publication/341766609_Privatization_and_Pandemic_A_Cross-Country_Analysis_of_COVID-19_Rates_and_Health-Care_Financing_Structures.

Barrientos, Armando, and Claudio Santibáñez. "New Forms of Social Assistance and the Evolution of Social Protection in Latin America." *Journal of Latin American Studies* 41, no. 1 (February 2009): 1–26.

Beech, Hannah, Alissa J. Rubin, Anatoly Kurmanaev, and Ruth Maclean. "The Covid-19 Riddle: Why Does the Virus Wallop Some Places and Spare Others?" *The New York Times*, May 3, 2020. www.nytimes.com/2020/05/03/world/asia/coronavirus-spread-where-why.html.

Berkley, Seth, et al. "World Development Report 1993: Investing in Health." *The World Bank*, 1993. https://documents.worldbank.org/en/publication/documents-reports/documentdetail/468831468340807129/world-development-report-1993-investing-in-health.

Blackman, Allen, et al. "Public Policy to Tackle Covid-19: Recommendations for Latin America and the Caribbean." *Inter-American Development Bank*, April 2020. https://publications.iadb.org/en/public-policy-to-tackle-covid-19-recommendations-for – latin-america-and-the-caribbean.

Blyth, Mark. *Austerity: The History of a Dangerous Idea*. Oxford: Oxford University Press, 2013.

Borges, Fabián A. "Neoliberalism with a Human Face? Ideology and the Diffusion of Latin America's Conditional Cash Transfers." *Comparative Politics* 50, no. 2 (January 2018): 147–67.

Briggs, Asa. "The Welfare State in Historical Perspective." In *The Welfare State Reader*, edited by Christopher Pierson and Francis G. Castles. Cambridge: Polity, 2006.

Cypher, James M., and James L. Dietz. *The Process of Economic Development*. New York: Routledge, 1997.

ECLAC. "Latin America and the Caribbean and the COVID-19 Pandemic: Economic and Social Effects." *Economic Comission for Latin America and the Caribbean*, April 3, 2020a. www.cepal.org/en/publications/45351-latin-america-and-caribbean-and-covid-19-pandemic-economic-and-social-effects.

ECLAC. "The Social Challenge in Times of COVID-19." *Economic Commission for Latin America and the Caribbean*, May 12, 2020b. www.cepal.org/en/publications/45544-social-challenge-times-covid-19.

El Espectador. "Cuatro proyectos que abren el debate sobre la renta básica universal en Colombia." *El Espectador*, July 28, 2020. www.elespectador.com/noticias/politica/renta-basica-universal-en-colombia-cuatro-proyectos-de-ley-que-abren-el-debate/.

Esteves, Roberto J. "The Quest for Equity in Latin America: A Comparative Analysis of the Health Care Reforms in Brazil and Colombia." *International Journal for Equity in Health* 11, no. 6 (February 2012). https://doi.org/10.1186/1475-9276-11-6.

García Márquez, Gabriel. *One Hundred Years of Solitude*. Edited by Gregory Rabassa. New York: Harper Perennial, 2006.

Gargarella, Roberto. "The Fight Against COVID-19 in Argentina: Executive vs Legislative Branch," May 1, 2020. https://verfassungsblog.de/the-fight-against-covid-19-in-argentina-executive-vs-legislative-branch/.

Giovanella, Ligia, and Mariana Faria. "Health Policy Reform in South America." In *The Palgrave International Handbook of Healthcare Policy and Governance*, edited by R. H. Blank, I. L. Bourgeault, C. Wendt, and E. Kuhlmann. London: Palgrave Macmillan, 2015.

Gobierno de Colombia. "Gobierno Nacional acelera la entrega de apoyos sociales a sectores más vulnerables, ante emergencia por el coronavirus COVID-19," March 27, 2020. https://id.presidencia.gov.co/Paginas/prensa/2020/Gobierno-Nacional-acelera-entrega-apoyos-sociales-sectores-mas-vulnerables-ante-emergencia-por-coronavirus-COVID-19–200327.aspx.

Haggard, Stephan, and Robert R. Kaufman. *Development, Democracy, and Welfare States: Latin America, East Asia, and Eastern Europe*. Princeton: Princeton University Press, 2008.

Hansing, Katrin, and Bert Hoffmann. "Cuba's New Social Structure: Assessing the Re-Stratification of Cuban Society 60 Years after Revolution." *German Institute of Global and Area Studies (GIGA) Working Papers*, February 2019.

Hoyos-Ceballos, Esteban, and Julián Gaviria-Mira. "Pandemic and Executive Powers in Colombia: A Problem and a Modest Proposal," April 17, 2020. https://verfassungsblog.de/pandemic-and-executive-powers-in-colombia-a-problem-and-a-modest-proposal/.

Londoño, Ernesto, Manuela Andreoni, and Letícia Casado. "President Bolsonaro of Brazil Tests Positive for Coronavirus." *The New York Times*, July 7, 2020. www.nytimes.com/2020/07/07/world/americas/brazil-bolsonaro-coronavirus.html.

López-Calva, Luis Felipe. "Inclusion Requires Capacity: The Role of Social Registries in Expanding Cash Transfers in the Wake of COVID-19," September 3, 2020. www.latinamerica.undp.org/content/rblac/en/home/presscenter/director-s-graph-for-thought/inclusion-requires-capacity – the-role-of-social-registries-in-e.html.

Malamud, Carlos, and Rogelio Núñez. "The Coronavirus Crisis in Latin America: Increased Presidential Power without Solid Foundations," April 14, 2020. www.realinstitutoelcano.org/wps/portal/rielcano_en/contenido?WCM_GLOBAL_

CONTEXT=/elcano/elcano_in/zonas_in/ari45-2020-malamud-nunez-coronavirus-crisis-in-latin-america-increased-presidential-power-without-solid-foundations.

Mesa-Lago, Carmelo. "The Cuban Welfare State System: With Special Reference to Universalism." In *The Routledge International Handbook to Welfare State Systems*, edited by Christian Aspalter, 106–21. London: Routledge, 2017.

Ministerio de Economía – Gobierno de Argentina. "Argentina.gob.ar," March 23, 2020. www.argentina.gob.ar/noticias/covid-19-el-gobierno-implementara-el-ingreso-familiar-de-emergencia-ife-para-aliviar-la.

Phillips, Tom. "'So what?': Bolsonaro Shrugs off Brazil's Rising Coronavirus Death Toll." *The Guardian*, April 29, 2020. www.theguardian.com/world/2020/apr/29/so-what-bolsonaro-shrugs-off-brazil-rising-coronavirus-death-toll.

Ulloa, Cristopher. "Sebastián Piñera anuncia nuevas medidas económicas para enfrentar al coronavirus en Chile." *CNN*, April 8, 2020. https://cnnespanol.cnn.com/2020/04/08/alerta-chile-pinera-anuncia-nuevas-medidas-economicas-para-enfrentar-al-coronavirus-2/.

United Nations. "Policy Brief: The Impact of COVID-19 on Latin America and the Caribbean." *United Nations Sustainable Development Group*, July 2020. https://unsdg.un.org/resources/policy-brief-impact-covid-19-latin-america-and-aribbean.

Uriarte-Gaston, Miren. "Social Policy Responses to Cuba's Economic Crisis of the 1990s." *Cuban Studies* 35 (2004): 105–36.

Valencia, Enrique. "Conditional Cash Transfers as Social Policy in Latin America: An Assessment of their Contributions and Limitations." *Anual Review oof Sociology* 34 (2008): 475–98.

Vargas, Arturo, and Claudio A. Méndez. "Health Care Privatization in Latin America: Comparing Divergent Privatization Approaches in Chile, Colombia, and Mexico." *Journal of Health Politics, Policy and Law* (Duke University Press) 39, no. 4 (May 2014): 841–86.

Waitzkin, Howard. *Health Care Under the Knife: Moving Beyond Capitalism for Our Health*. New York: Monthly Review Press, 2018.

Waitzkin, Howard, and Ida Hellander. "Obamacare: The Neoliberal Model Comes Home to Roost in the United States – If We Let It." In *Health Care Under the Knife: Moving Beyond Capitalism for Our Health*, edited by Howard Waitzkin. New York: Monthly Review Press, 2018.

5   Unpacking the multiple views of law

In the novel *One Hundred Years of Solitude*, Gabriel García Márquez sets forth a critique of the role of law. For him, both law and lawyers serve the interests of the ruling elite and have not only justified the existing status quo but have been complicit in aiding exclusion and dispossession. During the strike against the United Fruit Company, lawyers were able to erase the claims for better labor conditions advanced by the workers:

> The decrepit lawyers dressed in black who during other times had besieged Colonel Aureliano Buendia and who now were controlled by the banana company dismissed those demands with decisions that seemed like acts of magic. . . .
>
> Tired of hermeneutical delirium, the workers turned away from the authorities in Macondo and brought their complaints up to the higher courts. It was there that the sleight-of-hand lawyers proved that the demands lacked all validity for the simple reason that the banana company did not have, never had had, and never would have any workers in its service because they were all hired on a temporary and occasional basis. So that the fable of the Virginia Ham was nonsense, the same as that of the miraculous pills and the Yuletide toilets, and by a decision of the court it was established and set down in solemn decrees that the workers did not exist.
>
> (García Márquez 1970)

This last chapter brings together the insights provided by previous ones in order to explore the relationship between law and social transformation. The interpretation set forth in this chapter distances itself from the Marxist perspective illustrated by *One Hundred Years of Solitude*.[1] This Marxist perspective argues that law is structurally biased because it is a tool deployed to dominate and exploit the working class. Therefore, and according to this critique, the legal system is not only complicit in stacking the deck against the downtrodden, the disenfranchised, but also irrelevant, because it is determined and shaped by the forces of production. This last section of the book also distances itself from the belief in law's neutrality. Neutrality, it is argued, comes from the fact that laws are a set of instruments democratically debated and formally passed by congress. They are tools to arbitrate human interaction (as in the case of contracts and property) or mechanisms to promote social transformation (as in the case of decriminalizing abortion or allowing same-sex marriage), and as such reflect a plurality of social interests at a specific moment in history. For this theoretical frame, if law is complicit in the creation of inequality it has to do with bad legislation; a congress coopted by certain economic actors or corrupted in some way; a gap between the law in the books and the law in action or a lack of political will on the part of the ruling elites. Finally, this text opposes the view that by changing one set of laws, significant transformations will directly follow.

As the different chapters illustrate and this section brings together, it is important to explore what is left out of the picture when we imagine that the text of the law or the constitution will be able to transform society. I argue that the relevant rules to deal with a specific problem are not limited to a single legal field or topic. In fact, legal architecture is composed of layer after layer of reforms and regulations. Partly for this reason, but also because of historical context, economic background and the geopolitical space a country occupies, it is an impossible feat to separate the public from the private, contracts from criminal law, family law from labor law and the local from the global. In addition, the content of law is a product of a dynamic relationship, an ongoing struggle[2] over meaning. Therefore, law is not a static set of rules that are clearly written, applied in a consistent and predictable way. Rather, it is a battlefield where at any given moment, there are competing interpretations; actors who are trying to promote their particular vision of what it should be; institutions filled with bureaucrats who have discretionary power to decide its content and judges who will disentangle its meaning differently according to their ideological framework.

In sum, law is neither a direct instrument to promote change nor an impartial, neutral frame. It is not a rigid cage, either, that leaves no space for action. Rather, what this final chapter is proposing is that law is indeterminate, it entails more bargaining than adjudication, it is shaped by many forces as well as diverse rules and as a consequence is foundational to the distribution of resources. This view of law is more attuned with what Janet Halley (Halley et al. 2018) and others have called distributional analysis:

> The chief advantage of distributional analysis is that it is oriented not to the symbolic "norm announcing" function of law and legal institutions but to their distributional consequences. It asks of any particular

element of governance: *what distribution does it leave in place and what distributions does it shift?* Attempting to see distributions enables one to imagine *re*distributions.

(Halley, Conclusion Distribution and Decision Assessing Governance Feminism 2018)

Specifically in relation to law and development (represented by the dialogue between economic technocrats and lawyers) there is a range of theoretical interactions happening, which make the translation of objectives much more complex.[3] In order to lay out the traditional approaches to the field along with a more nuanced understanding of it, this last chapter has two sections. In the first one, I analyze diverse interpretations of the role of law in development by providing examples from diverse chapters in the book. The second part lays out the characteristics of the dynamic, interactive approach I am proposing.

The relationship between economic development and law: traditional approaches

The literature regarding law and development has explored this interaction extensively. How exactly should this relationship take place has been highly debated since the second half of the twentieth century (Trubek and Galanter, Scholars in Self-Estrangement: Some Reflections on the Crisis in Law and Development Studies in the United States 1974) (Trubek and Santos, The New Law and Economic Development: A Critical Appraisal 2006) (Trubek et al. 2014) (Trebilcock and Mota Prado 2019) (Kennedy and Stiglitz, Law and Economics With Chinese Characteristics 2013) (Alviar Garcia, Rethinking Law and Development in Colombia: How a Dynamic Approach Could Overcome the Chasm Between Law and Ideas of Economic Development 2016). The field has been characterized by searching for the answers to questions such as: Should law be an instrument for economic development? Is economic development intimately linked to a specific view of law? When does law promote or hinder economic development? These queries are important not only from a purely academic or theoretical perspective but they have also been extremely relevant for policy makers in the Third World, generally, and in Latin America, particularly.

In moving toward understanding the relationship between law and development, there have been, broadly speaking, two methods. The first one, I will call the law at the service of other goals. This approach assumes that economic or social ideals can be easily translated into legal tools and institutions. These include sweeping constitutional reforms and corresponding legal as well as administrative regulation. Specifically, and in relation to economic growth, a strengthening of the technocratic executive branch, which would intervene in the economy through modern administrative law, was deemed essential. In previous research, I have described how these ideas travelled in the Colombian context:

> Under the motto "less politics, more administration" it was believed that technocrats could structure and direct state institutions. Following this view, the administrative law reform of 1968 tried to promote a more centralized "apolitical" technocratic institutional setting through the creation of state enterprises and the strengthening of the government in order to direct economic matters.
> [. . .]
> As a consequence, the 1968 reform considerably broadened and strengthened the power of the executive branch. One of the reforms that increased the government's power to intervene broadly in different sectors of the economy either to prevent crises or simply to promote development plans. During periods of economic or social upheaval, the President could also use emergency measures to raise taxes and adopt a wide range of economic plans. This reform also widened the scope of governmental authority by giving the President control over the national budget, taxes and public spending. It made economic planning constitutionally mandatory. Through planning, the state controlled the production, distribution and demand of certain goods. It also controlled the minimal wage and salary levels in public enterprises, which affected private salaries as well. Finally, it allowed the President to directly intervene in the functioning of the Central Bank.
>
> (Alviar Garcia, Rethinking Law and Development in
> Colombia: How a Dynamic Approach Could Overcome the Chasm
> Between Law and Ideas of Economic Development 2016)

Then, there is the law-centered approach, where the goal is to solely transform the legal system and endow it with a set of institutions, which, once set in place, will provide the conditions to trigger economic growth. This law-centered approach has a liberal legalist perspective and a market-centered one. The liberal legalist perspective was promoted by early law and development movement scholars.[4] It advised governments in favor of an overhaul of the legal system, which included the strengthening of liberal values such as a clear separation of powers, formal equality and judicial autonomy.

Within the law-centered approach, there is also a market-focused perspective. It is different from the liberal legalist one in that it is not aimed at boosting state intervention or a technocratic executive branch; rather its goal is to strengthen private law (in the form of contracts and the protection of property rights) in order to guarantee the adequate flow of market transactions. Here, the centrality of law is exemplified by the Rule of Law project promoted by the World Bank as well as property formalization initiatives also advanced by multilateral institutions. This model entails a critique of what was understood as the excesses of a powerful executive and administrative regulation. Along these same lines, part of the reforms included a strengthening of the role of judges in order to protect individual rights, secure contracts and restrain the state from intervening in economic activities.

Law at the service of other goals

Many policy makers in Latin America have understood that economic development goals can be easily translated into legal instruments. In a way, this perspective assumes that law is a malleable device that can easily contain broader economic development objectives. From this point of view, whatever the definition of development is – import substitution industrialization or export-led growth – should be the guiding principles for development policies and the legal system should reflect this. David Kennedy describes this view in the following terms:

> The relative invisibility of law reflected the common assumption that law had little potential as an independent variable for generating development. Law was a tool for development policy makers, and as the instrument of economic policy, law was assumed to work more or less as advertised.
>
> (Kennedy, Law and Development Economics:
> Toward a New Alliance 2013)

As a consequence, the transformations that were needed are set forth mainly through administrative law and are not viewed in interaction within the legal environment. In addition, it was assumed that because technocrats have a more precise knowledge about economic development goals, the other branches of government should be deferent to their policy design.[5] An instrumental approach was also central to the tenants of the Cuban revolution. A strong administrative branch intervened in most aspects of the economy in order to promote export-led growth.

One example of this use of law can be found in the interaction between import substitution industrialization and access to property. As discussed in Chapter 2, in many countries in the region the social function of property was enshrined in order to aid import substitution industrialization. Land reform was an integral component of import substitution industrialization (ISI). Property distribution was necessary in order to achieve some form of poverty alleviation and provide resources for rural workers to consume the goods being produced by protected, local industries. At the same time, workers were needed in urban, industrial settings, which was achieved by mechanizing agricultural production and forcing the migration of peasants. In Colombia, and since 1936, property is defined as a social function that entails obligations, and several Constitutional Court rulings have reiterated this distributive impulse.

In Cuba, export-led growth was aided through the social function of property as well. As developed in the same chapter, the goal of agrarian reforms in Dependency inspired governments was to attack land concentration and facilitate state control over the production, distribution and export of commodities such as sugar. The Cuban Constitution of 1940 greatly limits private ownership to public interest and collective social interest.

This long-lasting faith in constitutional reform is also illustrated in Chapter 1 when analyzing the regulation of foreign investment in constitutional texts. The different countries analyzed provide not only contrasting concepts of what economic development means but also ideas of what a constitution, and the law, can achieve. In Bolivia, Evo Morales campaigned for years against neoliberal economic policies, which he claimed enriched a small transnational elite and impoverished the indigenous majority. Against the idea of universality and neutrality of traditional economic development models centered upon growth, the Bolivian Constitution included the incorporation of previously silenced ways of living and understanding progress and aimed to re-found the nation around novel social, political and economic ideas. In Venezuela, with the same faith in constitutional provisions, the first announcement president Hugo Chávez made upon assuming power was to propose not one but three referendums. Seven years later, Chávez sought to reform the constitution once again in order to, in his own words, consolidate the socialist state. Unable to change the constitution through a referendum, Chávez used a provision that allowed him to replace the legislative branch in certain matters and legislate. In Colombia, the constitution has been reformed more than 25 times, many of them geared to Constitutional Court rulings that interpreted the neoliberal content of the constitution within the frame of social and economic rights, effectively limiting the power of the market.

A final example of this approach can also be found in Chapter 3 where the enshrinement of equality has been central to feminist conquests both in Colombia and Bolivia. In Colombia, the constitution contains a number of articles aimed at reaching equality between men and women.[6] These constitutional provisions have been developed in multiple laws and regulations, which have been set in place in order to protect women's access to resources and economic development policies. These include quotas, the criminalization of violence against women and the reiteration of equal pay for equal work. In Bolivia, despite calls from the indigenous women's movement for a feminism more attuned with the idea of complementarity among genders, the constitutional provisions are more centered upon equality and nondiscrimination. Finally, in Cuba, the constitution also establishes equal rights for men and women and takes into account the interaction between productive and reproductive spheres by demanding that within the family the care of children should be shared equally.

Legal transformation as a goal on its own

Liberal legalism

Another way of interpreting the role of law in economic development was by arguing that legal transformation on its own was necessary for economic progress.[7] According to this liberal legal version, the establishment of a democratic system characterized by formal equality and separation of powers was necessary in order to reach economic development. The set of required reforms were not linked directly to economic development goals or definitions. In most countries of Latin America, import substitution industrialization was the predominant development road. Despite the diverse public policy avenues to achieve this economic model, the corresponding legal architecture should have some minimum characteristics: a system where there is formal equality; citizens influence and participate in legal design through the electoral process and a representative democracy; there are three branches of government and there is a strong system of checks and balances; judges adjudicate according to the clearly established rules.

In order to modernize law, future lawyers in charge of policy making needed to have a specific set of tools. As a consequence, there were many projects set in place in Latin American countries aimed at changing the way that law was thought of and taught. For example, USAID and the Ford Foundation promoted a range of legal education reforms during the 1960s in Asia, Africa and Latin America (mostly in Chile, Brazil and Colombia). I have described this transformation in the Colombian legal education and other related proposals in the following terms:

> Specifically, the objective was to transform the understanding and interpretation of law from a closed, rigid system to an open, flexible one that is influenced and transformed by social needs, economic

objectives and public policy choices. In this sense and given the depth and complexity of development policies aimed at state led industrialization and redistribution, the transformation of traditional legal education was necessary.

(. . .)

These proposals were directed toward the institutional organization of law schools, the curriculum, the teaching methods, and the goals of legal education. The reforms were in reaction to the general sense that law schools were failing to provide students with adequate knowledge of their social and cultural context and were not adapting to the contemporary needs of a developing society. It was thought that the reforms would produce a revitalized law school that equipped its graduates with greater reasoning skills, greater capacity for comprehension of their role in problem solving, and an acute sense of the law's relationship to social interests, values and systems.

(Alviar Garcia, The Classroom and the Clinic:
The Relationship between Clinical Legal Education,
Economic Development and Social Transformation 2008)

Centering the market

Establishing the legal framework to aid market transactions was in part a response to the state intervention model of the 1960s. This included a weakening of executive power typical of the developmental state; a privatization of state-owned enterprises and public services such as health and sanitation; a diminishment of state spending. Moreover, this period is characterized by revisiting and reinforcing of the idea that legal transformation was desirable on its own. An example of this is the increasing interest and research led by the World Bank regarding the relation between rule of law and development.[8]

In its setting out of the idea that legal reform was a necessary precondition for economic development, the bank stated that the 1960s experiment had failed because of a lack of an adequate theoretical underpinning. Starting the 1990s, this link was strongly supported with the insights provided by institutional economics (North 1991). In very broad terms, this meant that Third World countries would enhance development if a set of institutions worked efficiently.[9] One of these institutions was a functioning judiciary.

What was understood as meaningful legal institutions was different from the description of the liberal legalist model described earlier. This neoliberal version of legal transformation included the strengthening of private law[10] in order to secure transactions and avoid legal unpredictability, the guarantee of clear property rights (Brandt et al. 2002), increasing the importance of judges in order to restrain the state and facilitate the functioning of the market.

The formalization of property, as discussed in Chapter 2, is a good example of the strengthening of private law to improve the functioning of the market of urban or rural property. As a consequence, countries in the region with vast, productive and underused lands (in and near the Amazon, for example) became the focus of legal reforms to promote property formalization in order to aid plot accumulation necessary for agrobusiness. Multilateral institutions such as the World Bank argued that a road out of poverty would be paved by creating a nation of property owners. According to this initiative, if people had titles, they could use their homes as collateral for loans, which in turn would provide the seed for small businesses, thus unleashing the potential of capital, as Hernando de Soto would put it (De Soto 2001).

The interactive, dynamic approach

This interaction between ideas about law and its role in society with economic development goals is constantly evolving. The changes come from shifts in laws, institutions, styles of legal reasoning, and their encounter with market-oriented ideas of development or state-led industrialization. The relationship between law and economic development continues to be an elusive topic, notwithstanding the different perspectives described earlier. In my opinion, there is a range of interactions taking place that have not been adequately analyzed, and for this reason I propose unpacking this relationship with a set of tools that foreground the theoretical dialogue taking place between economists and lawyers.

First, it is essential to understand the basic assumptions that both lawyers and economists have about law and how these assumptions create biases and distribute resources. Lawyers and economists discussing ideas about economic development come from different theoretical traditions. They may be classical liberals, who believe in a clear separation of powers and a minimal state; they may be discrete interventionists who have faith in the capacity of government to promote economic and social change in order to correct historical circumstances that have temporarily prevented citizens from participating in the market; or they may be strong interventionist who want to deploy the power of the state to radically transform colonial legacies, dependency on developed nations and national distribution of power and resources. Interpreting where the terms of the ideological debate taking place is essential to politicizing debates that are presented as technical and demonstrating that there is nothing natural or inevitable about economic development definitions and goals, they are choices. The first four chapters of this book are designed to illustrate the terms of these theoretical debates. Second, the dialogue between legal and economic theory is far from seamless. Technocrats, policy makers and lawyers have different views about the role of law in society. Pinning down what idea of law is in the background of debates is essential to unveiling in what terms the struggle is taking place and surfacing the tensions not just between lawyers and economic technocrats but also among them. Some of the elements we should explore when describing these different views of law include background definitions of liberty and equality, the state and the market; historical and theoretical shifts regarding who should lead the redistribution of power and resources – should it be the legislative branch because it is more democratic, the executive because it is more technical, or the judiciary because it is counter majoritarian?

Third, it is necessary to explore the multiple ways in which law structures the market. In the US legal tradition, Robert Hale[11] was one of the first legal theorists to explain to what extent the market is not a natural entity but is determined by legal entitlements that are far from neutral. Rules such as those that regulate access to property; facilitate contracts; promote free trade or protectionist measures; frame family relations, including rules about divorce; define formal and informal workers or enable criminal law to protect of property or prohibit vagrancy, all determine the negotiating power of workers and owners alike.[12]

Fourth, a detailed description of the interaction among the different branches of government when targeting a development policy is required. This means understanding the ways in which legislators, judges and members of the executive branch act in order to structure a specific goal. Within this description, it is important to foreground the choices that policy makers, legislators and judges make about the best way to reach a specific development objective. For example, it is not obvious that a development policy should be naturally pursued through administrative law. It could be designed as the creation of a set of incentives in the private sphere. Within this interaction, it is important to unfold the contradictions and clashes between economic policy goals and constitutional provisions such as social and economic rights. This tool is particularly important in contemporary Latin America. In fact, while the 1980s and 1990s can be characterized by the globalization of the neoliberal project of the Rule of Law, the globalization of a neo-constitutionalist project must also be acknowledged (Rodríguez 2009). Constitutional tribunals in Latin America developed a strong presence in relation to social and economic rights (Rodríguez 2009). As described earlier, during the 1990s, one of the economic development goals was to reduce the size of the state, weaken its role in the distribution of resources and understand the market as the most efficient and neutral way to allocate goods in society. Even though this was the development goal, the removal of welfare style type policies faced important constitutional restrictions in many countries of the region. Privatization and the elimination of subsidies were framed within constitutions that included a generous bill of social and economic rights. Therefore, social and economic rights, including special provisions that demand from the state an obligation to guarantee human dignity and provide education, health and access to property to all the population provide a backdrop against which minimal state policies interact.

Diverse aspects of the chapters in this book include this dynamic approach. The analysis of the ideological choices made by governments on the left, center and right to deal with the regulation of direct foreign investment, property concentration, gender inclusion and welfare provisions are a first step in understanding the terms of the struggle. On the other hand, the centrality of constitutional or administrative law and its limitations are laid out in most chapters, along with the porous boundaries of relying simply on private law to guarantee entry to the market. The ongoing influence of background rules such as familial relations and access to resources in the case of female workers illustrates this interaction. Finally, local design of law and development policies are embedded in a global economic system, which will limit available governmental choices. This was the case in Cuba with state-managed sugar production and its corresponding property scheme after the fall of the Soviet Union coupled with the US embargo. It is also the case in countries influenced by neoliberal goals of export-led growth and the resource decline it brought, leaving Latin American countries dependent on exports with little resources to battle the Covid-19 pandemic.

Notes

1 For a more detailed analysis of the relationship between law and literature, see the introduction to this book and Helena Alviar Garcia, *Narración y Derecho, Derecho y Narración* (forthcoming).

2 David Kennedy, in his brilliant analysis of the global political economy in his book *A World of Struggle*, meticulously analyzes the contours of the legal struggle and explains at length what is at stake: "People struggle over these legal arrangements because they matter. Because law consolidates winnings, translating victory into right, legal entitlements are often the stakes as well as the tools for political and economic struggle. The status of forces or balance of power between groups and social interests – debtors and creditors, importers and exporters, state traders and multinationals, local labor and global capital, military powers and their insurgent opponents, is written in law and the relative leverage of economic or political competitors is rooted in the background legal and institutional structures within which people bargain and compete." David Kennedy, *A World of Struggle: How Power, Law, and Expertise Shape Global Political Economy* (Princeton: Princeton University Press, 2016), 11.

3 I take the word translation as an insight provided by David Kennedy in his article "Law and Development Economics: Toward a New Alliance." According to Kennedy, the use of the world translation foregrounds the difficulties that must be surpassed in order to apply any legal or economic goal. David Kennedy, "Law and Development Economics: Toward a New Alliance," in *Law and Economics With Chinese Characteristics*, ed. David Kennedy and Joseph Stiglitz (Oxford: Oxford University Press, 2013), 7.

4 Law and development scholars David Trubek and Marc Galanter explain the liberal legalist model in the following terms: "The liberal legalist model is a general model that explains the relationship between law and society and specifically explains the how legal systems and development relate. It contains six basic characteristics: 1) Society consists of individuals, intermediates and the State. The State has the power to coerce individuals and works through individuals. Both the State and intermediates are instruments used by individuals whom pursue their own welfare. 2) The State controls individuals through law. It does so, according to rules through which the State itself is coerced. 3) Rules are designed to achieve social purposes or attain social principles, in a conscious way. The rule making process is pluralist and there is no systematic advantage of some population over another. Intermediates are the principal actors in the rule-making process because they aggregate individual interests. 4) Rules are equally enforced for all citizens. 5) The legal order applies, interprets and changes universalistic rules. The central institutions of the legal order are Courts, which have the final saying in defining the social significance of law. The typical decisive mode of legal action is adjudication, which follows authoritative rules and doctrine as its outcome. 6) The behavior of social actors tends to follow the rules. When the population does not comply with the rules, officials will enforce them." David M. Trubek and Marc Galanter, "Scholaris in Self-Estrangement: Some Reflections on the Crisis in Law and Development Studies in the United States," *Wisconsin Law Review* (1974): 1062–103.

5 David Trubek describes this approach as follows: "In the 1960s, development economist favored a strong role of the state, believed that private enterprise lacked the resources to build key industries and that state ownership was essential, and thought that import substitution industrialization and delinking from world markets was the preferred road to development. (. . .) Law and development accepted the need for a strong state and drew on prevailing ideas about the power of public law as a transformative agent." David M. Trubek, Helena Alviar Garcia, Diogo R. Coutinho, and Alvaro Santos, *Law and the New Developmental State: The Brazilian Experience in Latin American Context* (New York: Cambridge University Press, 2014), 5.

6 Articles 13, 43, 64, 65, 80.

7 This idea was inspired by Weber's analysis of the role of law in industrialization and modernization. For more see David M. Trubek, "Max Weber and the Rise of Capitalism," *Wisconsin Law Review* (1972): 720–53.

8 The rule of law was greatly boosted by the World Bank, "in the 1990s there was a message surge in development assistance for law reform projects in developing and transition economies involving of many billions of dollars. The World Bank alone reports that it has supported 330 'rule of law' projects and spent $2.9 billion on this sector since 1990." Michael Trebilcock and Ronald J. Daniels, *Rule of Law Reform and Development* (Northhampton: Edward Elgar, 2008), 2.

9 Thomas Biersteker illustrates the influences of the World Bank and the IMF in the reduction of the state. He describes that "One way for a government to accomplish fiscal adjustment is for it to reduce its deficits, both by reducing current spending and improving the efficiency of its investments. For this reason, the former president of the World Bank, A.W. Clausen, applauded the government of Ghana for laying off 18,000 employees." Thomas Biersteker, "Reducing the Role of the State in the Economy: A Conceptual Exploration of the IMF and World Bank Prescriptions," *International Studies Quarterly* (1990): 477–92.

10 David Trubek and Alvaro Santos point out that the "Second Moment legal reforms were designed to strengthen the rights of property and ensure that contracts would be enforceable. Emphasis was placed on the role of the judiciary both as a way to restrain the state and to facilitate markets." David Trubek and Alvaro Santos, "Introduction: The Third Moment in Law and Development Theory and The Emergence of a New Critical Practice," in *The New Law and Economic Development: A Critical Appraisal*, ed. David Trubek and Alvaro Santos (New York: Cambridge University Press, 2006), 6.

11 For a brilliant analysis of Robert Hale's work see Duncan Kennedy, "The Stakes of Law or Hale and Foucault," in *Sexy Dressing Etc. Essays on the Power and Politics of Cultural Identity*, ed. Duncan Kennedy (Cambridge: Harvard University Press, 1993), 83–125.

12 David Kennedy further explains how law structures the market in the following way: "The turn to law is important. Capital is after all, a legal institution – a set of entitlements to use, risk and profit from resources of various kinds. Law defines what it means to 'own' something and how one can successfully contract to buy or sell. Financial flows are also flows of legal rights. Labor is also a legal institution – a set of legal rights and privileges to bargain, to work under these and not those conditions, to quit, to migrate, to strike, to retire and more. Buying and selling are legal institutions-rooted in what it means to own or sell in a given legal culture, in the background legal arrangements in whose shadow people bargain with one another over price. Markets are built upon a foundation of legal arrangements and stabilized by a regulatory framework. Each of these many institutions and relationships can be defined in different ways – empowering different people and interests. Legal rules and institutions defining what it means to 'contract' for the sale of 'property' might be built to express quite different distributional choices and ideological commitments."

Bibliography

Alviar Garcia, Helena. *Narración y Derecho, Derecho y Narración,* Forthcoming.
Alviar Garcia, Helena. "The Classroom and the Clinic: The Relationship between Clinical Legal Education, Economic Development and Social Transformation." *UCLA Journal of International Law and Foreign Affairs* (2008): 206–7.
Biersteker, Thomas. "Reducing the Role of the State in the Economy: A Conceptual Exploration of the IMF and World Bank Prescriptions." *International Studies Quarterly* (1990): 477–92.
Brandt, Cfr, et al. "Land Rights in Rural China: Facts, Fictions and Issues." *The China Journal* (2002): 67–97.

De Soto, Hernando. "The Mystery of Capital." *International Monetary Fund, Financy and Development Magazine,* 2001.

García Márquez, Gabriel. *One Hundred Years of Solitude.* Translated by Gregory Rabassa. New York City: Harper and Row Publishers, 1970.

Duncan Kennedy "The Stakes of Law or Hale and Foucault." In *Sexy Dressing Etc. Essays on the Power and Politics of Cultural Identity,* Duncan Kennedy, 83–125. Cambridge: Harvard University Press, 1993.

Halley, Janet. "Conclusion Distribution and Decision Assessing Governance Feminism." In *Governance Feminism: An Introduction,* edited by Janet Halley, Praba Kotiswaran, Rachel Roubuche and Hila Shamir, 253. Minneapolis: University of Minnesota Press, 2018.

Halley, Janet, Prabba Kotiswaran, Rachel Rebouche, and Hila Shamir. *Governance Feminism: An Introduction.* Minneapolis: University of Minnesota Press, 2018.

Kennedy, David. *A World of Struggle: How Power, Law, and Expertise Shape Global Political Economy.* Princeton: Princeton University Press, 2016.

Kennedy, David. "Law and Development Economics: Toward a New Alliance." In *Law and Economics With Chinese Characteristics,* edited by David Kennedy and Joseph Stiglitz, 7. Oxford: Oxford University Press, 2013.

Kennedy, David, and Joseph E Stiglitz. *Law and Economics With Chinese Characteristics.* Oxford: Oxford University Press, 2013.

Rodríguez, César. *La globalización del Estado de Derecho. El neoconstitucionalismo, el neoliberalismo y la transformación institucional en América Latina.* Bogotá: Universidad de los Andes, 2009.

Trubek, David M. "Max Weber and the Rise of Capitalism." *Wisconsin Law Review* Wisc.L.Rev., no. 3 (1972): 720–753.

Trubek, David M., and Marc Galanter. "Scholaris in Self-Estrangement: Some Reflections on the Crisis in Law and Development Studies in the United States." *Wisconsin Law Review* (1974): 1062–103.

Trubek, David M., Helena Alviar Garcia, Diogo R. Coutinho, and Alvaro Santos. *Law and the New Developmental State: The Brazilian Experience in Latin American Context.* New York: Cambridge University Press, 2014.

Trubek, David M., and Alvaro Santos. "Introduction: The Third Moment in Law and Development Theory and The emergence of a New Critical Practice." In *The New Law and Economic Development: A Critical Appraisal,* edited by David Trubek and Alvaro Santos, 6. New York: Cambridge University Press, 2006.

Trubek, David M., and Alvaro Santos. *The New Law and Economic Development: A Critical Appraisal.* Cambridge: Cambridge University Press, 2006.

Index

Page numbers in **bold** indicate a table on the corresponding page.

Printed in the United States
by Baker & Taylor Publisher Services